SOCIAL DANCING

GUIDE FOR

BACHATA, KIZOMBA, SALSA, ZOUK

BEGINNERS GUIDE

ARE YOU READY FOR THE DANCE FLOOR?

BY

SAMBOU T. KAMISSOKO

Disclaimer

This book has been written for information purposes only. Every effort has been taken towards making this Book as true, complete and accurate as possible. However, there may be mistakes in typography or content. Also, this book provides information relevant on the different dance and the act of dance. Therefore, this Book should be used as a guide knowing that new information is constantly coming up. The purpose of this Book is to educate.

The author do not warrant that the information contained in this book is fully complete and shall not be responsible for any errors or omissions. The author shall have neither liability nor responsibility to any person or entity with respect to any loss or damage caused or alleged to be caused directly or indirectly by this book.

Dedication

Dedication to my first dance teacher in Charlotte NC, Muhammad Abdullah, AKA "cat in the hat". Without your continuous passion for partner dances, I wouldn't have stuck around in the dance world; you help, cemented the foundations for me and many others around in the dance communities.

I appreciate the flame you have ignited in me; ever since I met you. And that flame is everlasting burning in me. It has open up pathways of love, growth, creativity, sharing, excitements and a lot of fun times.

This book is a reflection of the chain of love that you built. And my wish is to share the love with many people all around the world. I thank you for all the beautiful words and inspirations you have shared.

Special Thanks To:

Mariah Cruz, Idriss Guindo Audi MPk, Mike Ahombi, Danielle Houston, William Case, Joy Gouger

I appreciate all of your contributions, directly or indirectly. You have played a great role in my social dancing experiences through social, classes and in the dance festivals. Your encouragements through the conversations we had have been helpful in writing this book. And your inputs and testimonials are a great example of your helpful hearts. I am very thankful for your support.

Sources Credit To:

Kimerer LaMothe Ph.D. Why Do Humans Dance. www.vitalartsmedia.com

March 31, 2015. 6/28/2018.

www.psychologytoday.com

Cheryl Cortez. How to Choose Ballroom Dance Shoes

04.06.2012. 01.21.2018.

www.arthurmurraydc.com

Michael Douglas. Dance Etiquette. 01.18.2014. 12.15.2017. www.salsa4life.com

Peter Hastie. What Is Social Dance. 2006. 10.23.2017. www.auburn.edu

www.heritageinstitute.com .Social Dancing 10.24.2017

Contents

Introduction 1

Part 1

The Definition, Essence, and Value of Social Dancing 3

The Culture of Social Dancing 8

What Is Social Dancing? 11

Why People Dance? 17

Real People And Their Experiences In The Social Dance World 24

Part 2

Few Types of Social Dances and Music 27

Level of Dancers 35

Followers (Follow) and Leaders (Lead) In Social Dancing 40

Part 3

How to Find Dance Classes and Events 43

Part 4

What Shoe To Wear? 51

Part 5

What To Wear/Bring 65

Classy Dancer 69

Part 6

First Time At The Social Dance Floor, New Social Dancer   75

How To Adjust To Your Partner?   78

Guide For Couple On Social Dancing   80

Part 7

How To Ask Someone To Dance With You: Ladies And Gentleman   85

Ladies, The Reasons He Did Not Invite You For A Dance   90

Men, Why A Lady Might Not Want To Dance With You   96

Part 8

Ways To Be A Better Dancer   101

Part 9

Types Of Dancers   115

Part 10

Habits To Be Avoided   125

Part 11

Other Dance Events To Attend   139

Social Dance Congress   139

Social Dance Festivals   140

Tips For Saving Money   149

Introduction

Welcome To The World Of Social Dancing

You spot her. There she is sitting among her girlfriends; somehow standing out from the rest. You think for just a second or two, she caught your eyes upon her, and she smiled. That was the clue and encouragement you were looking for. One more sip, and you manage to get on your feet and begin walking across the floor to ask her to dance.

You feel nervous and as you walk toward her, you feel as though every eye in the room was watching your every step. What if she was smiling at someone else, or just being kind? What if she says no? God, the embarrassment, and then the long walk back to my seat. I can hear my friends now: "what happened man? Boy did you get dissed. It's okay bro; she was looking at me anyway." Even though they mean it all in good fun to ease the pain of rejection, it does not help. Welcome to the world of social dancing.

With the possibility of such embarrassment from being rejected by a woman who chooses not to accept your invitation to dance, to the pain a woman feels who has gotten all dressed up to dance, and finds herself sitting as dance after dance goes by, or if asked to dance, it is by those she would prefer looked elsewhere the terrain of social dancing can seem very intimidating. Why then, would you even bother putting yourself under such pressure? You already have enough stress in your life.

The answer is simple. It is worth it. Over the pages to follow, Sambou will tell you why, and how to manage the journey in such a fashion as to get the wonderful experience that successful social dancing can be in your life.

To get you started, I will give you a glimpse of what is social dancing and why it is such a great journey to take. I will tell you more about Sambou, who has been one of my favorite students, who quickly emerged as one so talented and committed that I often called upon him to assist me both in the instruction of others and to demonstrate the dances we were teaching. It has been my honor to encourage him as he has continued his amazing dance and life journey.

Part 1

The Definition, Essence, and Value of Social Dancing

Although social dancing has some elements of performance, it is not primarily aimed at performance. Performance dancing, largely done by professionals, its primary purpose is to entertain or influence the viewing audience. By contrast, social dancing is primarily for the benefit of the dancers. It is rarely choreographed as much performance dancing usually is, but rather more spontaneous, flexible and in the moment.

The essence of dance is connection. If there is no connection, there is no dance. This connection is to the music and to your dancing partner. This is not the full extent of connection, but connecting to the music and to each other are the most important elements; particularly in maintaining that connection in the midst of spontaneity. Spontaneity is often where the excitement can be found, and what makes each dance unique.

The essence of connection requires for the dancers to be fully present. You have often seen where several people are having a meal, or engaged in some other group activity, but each person is on their cell phone or on some other electronic device. In such an instance, this means they are physically present, but their heart, mind, and soul is elsewhere. As such, they are not fully present. So being present not only makes the dance connection possible, but it teaches and trains you to do the same in life. Otherwise, not only is there no connection, there is no communication, and communication can't occur if you are not present.

Being present means you are listening to one another, and committed to staying present. In fact, the dance is a conversation. It is a conversation between the dancers. Even though in most partnership social dancing one person is leading (usually the man) and one person is following (usually the woman), it is a conversation, not a lecture. If you are lecturing, you are not listening. If you are lecturing, there is likely to be less enjoyment for your partner. A good leader is committed to the conversation, which means he is listening to his partner as to what is being received well and what pleases her. If he does this, they are communicating, and he will adjust as is necessary, and his partner will enjoy the dance.

He is creating "connection not tension." His partner will relax, trust him more, and her commitment to the dance will deepen. At the end of the dance, what your partner will remember most, is not all the fancy steps you tried to do, but how you made her feel. She will enjoy the dance, and want to dance with you again. Unbeknownst to you, she will tell her friends, how much she enjoyed dancing with you, and when that happens other ladies will want to dance with you too. The opposite is also true: if she did not enjoy the dance, she will spread that news as well. In essence, those who dance with you make your reputation as a dancer; your joy as a social dancer is in their hands.

The final key is to dance from the inside out, from your heart and soul. You have heard the expression, "his heart wasn't really in it." That means, while he did some act, he really didn't want too or he was only half doing it, as his heart and soul was missing. You are your heart and soul; your body is just your instrument.

I have emphasized to all my students and colleagues, that this is what separates the joy from merely going through the motions, the great dances from the average or good ones: put your heart and soul into it. If you do so, she will feel it.

This is one of the great benefits of social dancing. If you fully commit to the dance, the stresses of life fall away. If you fully commit to your partner's joy, you will have joy as well, and in the process you both elevate the dance you are sharing beyond the ordinary experiences of everyday life, and you may even reach a magical moment, a realm of such bliss and peace of mind, that you will wonder how did I ever not do this. This magical moment is the sweet spot of dancing. It is the addictive quality that calls you back again and again. It is one of the reasons why we dance.

Social dancing will bring into your life, people you might not ordinarily meet. Dance is the common ground, and as such brings comfortably together people of so many diverse cultures, races, ages, professions, languages, and background. I have seen dance all over the world, even danced with ladies whose language I could not speak. As I told my son, while the brain speaks many languages, the heart speaks them all.

If it were not for dance, I would not have met Sambou. What a lost that would have been. Sambou is from Mali, in West Africa. And as he would learn, Africa is at the root of so many dances, including Latin dance, which is one of the reasons, he so quickly grasped the many dances, I was blessed to share with him. He was a quick study, a great student, a greater friend, and very soon my right hand man who I often called upon to help me instruct and guide others.

We started our journey in Salsa, Bachata, Merengue, Cha-Cha-Cha, Argentine Tango, and even Kizomba. He passed through the corridors of all these dances, finding a very rich attachment to Kizomba, for which he has become well known. He not only participated in dance as both a dancer and a teacher, but he assisted me with putting on events, and very soon was doing many events of his own. At its core, his heart was not just about "Sambou," but also about sharing this wonderful experience with others.

Not surprisingly, you are experiencing an aspect of his sharing in this book you are now reading. I hope you will take the journey these many pages will walk you through. I am certain, his experience and insights will be valuable guidance for your consideration as you take this incredible journey of life. Welcome to the world of social dancing.

Thank you Sambou for giving back. I am so grateful and proud of the man you are, are becoming, and continuing to evolve to be, and for whatever positive part I have played in your journey.

Muhammad Abdullah, Dance de Soul

July, 2018

The Culture of Social Dancing

The culture of social dancing has been on for many generations and places, from the Americas to the coast of Africa. These dance places are the gateway to meet and greet people from different parts of the world. The culture of social dancing is full of joy, passion, laughter, love, and sharing. Social dancing is a lifestyle to many people, especially if you grew up in Latin America and a certain part of Africa. People gather to share their dance skills while enjoying refreshment around the street corner. Countries such as Angola, Cuba, Columbia, Brazil, and New York are a great example of a culture full of an abundance of social dancing around the street corners and local bars.

In North America, the culture of social dancing is charged with classes, workshops and events such as parties, festival congresses. Social dancing brings with it lots of fun, love, and diversity which makes it appealing to different demographics: you may meet someone from Europe, Africa, Latin America, and Asia, young and old all under one roof sharing their love for social dancing.

The friends you make can potentially be lifetime friends, because the hobby never dies, as long as you can walk you can dance. That is the mentality of most social dancers, it is a lifetime passion we grow with; while sharing the joy with new and familiar friends. It is part of our weekly routine to keep the skills sharpen. Serious social dancers attend at least one dance event per week in addition to the practice sessions. This may include classes, workshops or a practice with a friend of the same interest.

A social dancing event is filled with hours of dancing. Your local dance party duration is about a minimum of three hours of dancing; festival night social dances average about five to six hours of dancing per night. Festivals and Congress can be few days to a week-long of events; you might wonder how we do it? It could be the magic in the music. Social dancing creates a platform for its dancers to stay fit and is a major reason some people join this lifestyle in order to get and stay in great shape.

There are usually more Ladies than guys in social dancing events out-number the guys which can be attributed to the culture they grew up in. Many men in North America did not grow up attending social dancing schools and events in the street corners. Some of them are reluctant to loosen-up to social dancing and may feel it is a feminine thing to do. Ladies find it easier to try social dancing and according to a survey most of the new couples at a social dance floor were convinced by their lady to try it. That is true with dance dates and as a dance instructor specializing in dance dates, anytime I got a private class for a date; I always ask this question. "Whose idea was this"? The lady usually will respond is "mine"! 70 percent of the time ladies are the one who takes initiative to try social dancing. It is not a surprise why you may sometimes found 2:1 ratio female dancers to men on the dance floor. For that reason, male dancers are really appreciated on the dance floor, especially if you can lead precisely well. This gap also gives ladies the window to start leading while becoming better followers as well. These numbers depends on the locations as well.

In general, social dancing is a source of joy. No matter what happens or what is happening in your life, is important to leave your entire problem at the door before you leave your house. When you get to the dance floor, it is time to feed and ignite your passion. Your great energy is bliss to the dance floor, release it. That can go a long way. One way to generate great vibes on the dance floor is to meet & greet the folks you come in contact with. Take the effort to say "hi" to everyone when possible. With this manner, you can warm up the atmosphere within you and transfer it to whoever you dance with.

What Is Social Dancing?

Social dancing is a dance that involves partner dance which focuses on sociability and enjoyment of the moment between both dancers. The dance is meant for both partners to enjoy the music and each other. It is not a "show" but a game of connection and seduction. You do it for the love of the dance and satisfaction of the other partner, not the crowd. You dance from in and out like no one is watching. Simply being yourself.

Sociability and having fun are an important aspect of social dancing, without it the fun and tradition might be lost. Sociability involves the abilities to meet, greet, sharing your love of dance with new or familiar people. Unlike the traditional dance clubs, almost everybody in the social dance floor is in a social mode ready to dance per invitation.

Partner Dances

This is a dance with basics steps that are practice by two individual with each dancer playing a fundamental role.

It is common in partner dances to see a man lead and the lady follows. It has been said "it takes two to tango" that is exactly what a partner dance requires. However, non-partner dance such as a line-dance, Afro-house; sometimes blend in social dance floor to spice up the atmosphere. These dances are usually added to challenge your feet and it is common in dance festivals to add a little moment of a line dance during the social. It is a symbol of harmony that involves everyone's participation. These are the moments you can go wild to express your individuality like you don't care.

Social dancing does not require a large dance floor like ballroom dancing. Typical social dancing is done in pubs, studios, restaurants and even in the street corners in the communities no matter how crowded it is. Most social dances are very flexible and provide maximum freedom to express yourself as an individual. This dynamic nature of it provides a room to grow and evolve in time with the music without distorting the classical ones or the original. It is common as a beginner to get confused with which kind of dance to learn because music evolves in time. For example, Bachata dance has an extension called "sensual Bachata", Argentine Tango dance, has an extension called Tango Nuevo" "Kizomba dance, has an extension called Urban- Kizomba. Each country and individual has their own flavor added to the dance to express their individuality.

This is part of the reasons many dance instructors teach the steps and techniques differently. This characterizes the beauty and nature of dance, you will never get bored as long as you keep learning and growing with the dances. There is always a step to be discovered and to be shared.

Types of Social Dancing

Types of social can be described by the pattern of the moves. Based on the forms and patterns it can be categorized as Spot or Progressive Dances

Spot Social Dancing

These are dances that can be performed in a small dance space or in one area by the couples and does not require a large ballroom. Dancers involved in spot dances use small steps and close embrace for efficiency. That way, you may dance many hours with different partners efficiently. These are the common spot dances, Latin dances (Salsa, Bachata, Merengue, Rumba Tango Nuevo) Afro dances (Semba, Zouk, Kizomba) North America (West Coast and East Coast Swing)

Progressive Social Dancing

On the other hand, usually has a circular direction, it allows the dancer to travel in an anti- clockwise direction on the dance floor. These dances need a larger space than the spot to allow free flow with nature of the dance. In social, Progressive dancers use the edges of the dance floor to express the way of the dance in a circular form. This helps the partners to dance in an organized pattern. These are some of the common progressive dances, (Waltz, Country two steps, Foxtrot, Argentine Tango) Progressive can be classified as a ballroom or standard dances.

My First Social Dance

My first experience on social dancing was discouraging and promising. I remember picking up a phone and called a dance company about the salsa classes and events. And this lovely lady on the phone invited me to the social dancing & classes they were having that night. When I got there, I realized that the class was not designed for beginners even though it was supposed to start with an introductory class before the social. I opted to stay for the dance social which I found myself struggling with the moves without understanding the basics. I was overwhelmed tremendously; due to never taking a salsa dance class before. While trying to be sociable, I realized that most of the followers (ladies) weren't patient with me and had expectations of me to be their shining armored Knight to save their night which put me under massive pressure. It felt like being in a foreign land trying to communicate and nobody understood my language. I had to mask my frustration with a few smiles to still be sociable.

In the middle of frustration, a lady came to me with a dance invitation. I had to tell her that. "I am very new in salsa dancing", in other to release some of the pressure and expectations. She replied" that is ok" to my surprise, she was very patient with me. She even helped back lead a few basic steps to make it easier. After the dance, she then invited me to a New Year social party at her place. During the house party, I was able to meet an older gentleman called Muhammad Abdullah, "AKA cat in the hat" who introduced me into the fundamentals of salsa and musicality. Without the assistance of the lady and Muhammad's ability to articulate words nicely through his explanation of dance, and his continuous invitations to social dancing and classes; I would have given up after that first social dance experience. Sometimes the first impression can make or break a deal and sometimes it depends on how it ends.

That's part of the reasons I wrote this book. To share my experiences and understanding in other to help new dancers, beginners or pre dancers (potential dancers). So that when you found yourself with similar scenarios stated in this book; you should feel prepared to deal with it. With better tools and information, you can effectively prepare and enjoy the journey of social dancing.

Your progress is based on your level of commitment. With clarity and some effort, you can map your road to success in social dancing. This book provides information that is helpful to anybody who wants to get started and flourish in social dancing.

Yes! You can do it. A master was once a student. This new hobby is an art of connection, a Joy which it has brought to me and many other people that I met during this journey. Be open to the experience, designed by nature that will bring you joy, talents, skills, and love.

I hope this book would be helpful to get you started, equipped, gain and maintain a new hobby, and learn to express yourself fully while dancing.

Why People Dance?

Hotel California" one of the great eagle song, stated that "some people dance to remember and some dance to forget" or, it could be a combination of both. When you dance to "remember", you are dancing to create pleasant memories. Memories you can reflect on and enjoy it.

On the other hand, when you dance to "forget", you are dancing to override the old unpleasant memories that you may have encountered. In time with more pleasant dance experiences you can feel livelier and happier. When you look at it closely, you are always dancing to remember. Just initially your reasons can be different but the goals are the same. That is to create joyful experiences.

Certainly, dance can be a gateway to experience tremendous joy. It has the ability to heal past unpleasant moments.

According to Kimerer LaMothe Ph.D., a dancer, philosopher, and author of a book titled, "why we dance". She stated that: "Humans dance because dance is human. Dance is not an accidental or supplemental activity in which humans choose to engage or not. Dance is essential to our survival as human beings".

There are many reasons to dance; each one is personal for many dancers. However, you don't need a reason to dance. Because dance is innately in us, dance is being a full-blown human. Whether you pay attention or not, dance is part of your day to day routine. For example, a person sweeping the floor to a person surfing the ocean is dancing. A leaf of a tree moving with the wind is dance. Even a secretary in the office signing the papers, those simple acts contains dance. As you can see, these examples above have something in common, a flow of energy into the movements. Dance is a vital part of human existence. Dance is in you, you can't run away from it. All you need to do is to surrender to it and let it flow in and out without reasons. Unleash it; break that mask and express yourself fully. That is how dance moves are made, people trusting their inner impulses and translates them into patterns.

Dance doesn't need to have a meaning either, because each person has their own meaning. Definitely, the value it brings to you is undeniable. The question is why not giving it a big go? If dance is part of you, why not experience it in a deeper level?

Often when I ask people to dance with me, they reply "I have two left feet" That statement makes me laugh so hard. Being a non-native in North America, I couldn't wrap my head around it.

"How is that possible? I said to myself "Two left feet? Of course, I eventually got it. We are all born with rhythm. You just need to let it flow. Some just need, some, inspiration, influences to come out of their shells and start learning to dance in a particular way.

I found that some people found these common reasons to start dancing.

Dance To Heal

This is one of the most common answers I found form students. This answer is common with people in their forties and above. Either they are dancing to heal from the past or present trial in their life or some dance to stay healthy which is another form of healing.

This trial such as a disease, death or illness of a love one, or unpleasant event in people's life can trigger people to get out and look for answers out there. Part of the answer can be, "I need to live more". "I need to have fun", "I need to feel young and vibrant again". So, these folks have dancing in their bucket lists. The fact that most of them spend too much time in battling life's trials, the need to become livelier is necessary for their survival. This need for more fun lifestyle serves as a doorway to initiate dancing. They turned their life's around through social dancing, by taking a group class, private classes, workshops to gain fun and healing skills that will somehow be therapeutic to their life's.

Dancing To Get Fit Or Stay Fit

This reason is quite popular. Whether its Afro beats, Zumba, Salsa, people taking these classes have one common goal, get or stay fit. I met many dancers who have lost a lot of weight through salsa dancing. These dancers transformed their look for the better. They took many classes, workshops, and attended dance socials.

The fun fact is that you can burn over four hundred calories while dancing per hour. Imagine dancing for two to three hours straight in a weekly dance social. These socials are very common in dance communities. With a reasonable diet and a weekly dance schedule, many people have reached their goal of being fit and staying fit. Furthermore, the fun part is that; when dancing, it feels like there is no pain. Of course, you are moving and doing the work. It feels easier than gym because music and connection with people are involved. If you have never done social dancing before, try it for two hours. I bet the next morning you will feel some sort of soreness in a different part of your body. This is an indication of a whole body workout. The difference is that, with dancing, you are doing it wisely. It is a collective effort, which involves people, music, connection, and art. At the gym your mindset is to workout, this can make it harder for you. At social dancing places, your mindset is to have fun.

Dance To Get New Skills

Some people join dance classes mainly to acquire a new skill. These are the dancers who take their dancing to the next level. Such dancers are the one who eventually becomes teachers and professional dancers. These dancers usually start from zero and work their way to master the art of a particular dance. They are always active in classes, taking workshops, joining dance groups, to become better quickly as possible. Because they have a goal to reach, that can take a couple of years or more to achieve. They pace themselves and work their way up. These dancers are the one who stick around for a while. They consider dance as a lifetime journey; and are willing to explore it.

Dancing To Socialize

This is also very common as well. In social dancing, it is usual to meet a different kind of people, from all walks of life; exposing themselves to different kinds of music from many countries. This serves as a bridge to cultures, where people come socialize, network. Many first-timers come to enjoy the diversity in the room. The vibrant spirit on the social dance floor is amazing. You just have to experience it. People meet & greet each other. Strangers become familiars within minutes. People take off their mask and just dance. These dancers dance just for the fun of it.

Dance To Meet A Potential Partner

It is really beautiful when your new passion brought you a loved one. As years pass by, I observed many dancers, new or veteran formed romantic relations. Some of these relationships were short-term and some of it were long term. Of course, nothing lasts forever but the moments' matters. One of the benefits of social dancing is the ability to bring people together. This opens the opportunities for people to network, build connections.

There are a lot of singles ladies and men in the dance communities. Some of them are ready to meet someone special. So if you get your grooves right, you might get lucky. Enjoy the moment with your partner. Just respect the dance! If you found a partner through dancing, please don't let your passion for dance fade away in time. Keep in mind relationship is chemistry. Sometimes it might fade away and when it does, you are going to need something exciting such as dancing to hold it back together. Dance is a valuable skill to keep and maintain a relationship. If not, you might end up finding yourself on the dance floor finding another partner.

Furthermore, if you are here to find that special someone, learn to take it easy, avoid being needy or showing a sign of desperation. Enjoy the process, learn the dance, respect the dance, and try to master a particular dance. Keep in mind ladies love good dancer and the same is true for guys. The better dancer you become the more attractive you become on the dance floor. Honestly, that might help land a butterfly on your shoulder.

Whatever reason sparks you or even without any reason, the hardest part is making that initial move, taking that first step. Just do it, pick up that phone, call the dance studio, get on your social media, contact that dance group about the next class, attend that dance festival or even better schedule a private lesson for a fast track. I promised, once you discover the joy of dancing, you will wish you have done it sooner.

Real People And Their Experiences In The Social Dance World

Mariah Cruz

I started dancing because I was new to Charlotte and my first summer here I had no social connections to people outside of my job. Social dancing was the perfect opportunity to accomplish two goals meet people and learn salsa. This was a perfect combination in so many levels. Challenging myself to learn a dance and create friendships. I had no idea that a dancing community existed. These communities become my family!

The number one thing that I gained from joining the different social dance communities such as Tango, Kizomba and Salsa are the friendships I created. I have become and gained aunties, sisters, brothers and friends that I called when in need. My life is so rich because I am dancer. I can travel anywhere in the world and find a social or a class. People that are not dancers do not understand the commitment you need to make to become a good dancer. This commitment can be costly from classes and traveling to Festival and Congress but the joy from dancing is so immense. Sometimes, you can make a connection with a dancer, you move in harmony, and we enter our own world. No one exist only two people as one dancing in pure joy! The more you dance, the more you need to learn so I am a professional beginner. This hobby can become a big part of your life. As dancers, our favorite topics are when is the next social, when is the next festival, where to buy the best clothes for dancing. After all dancers, enjoy shopping for dance clothes and shoes work clothes is an afterthought. The music from these dances is my therapy. I am not having a good day, I can play my Salsa, Kizomba or Tango and I am in my happy place!

Would I recommend it to others? Absolutely! Dancing improves you in so many areas from physical aspects to mentally. If you are looking to invest in a life changing experience... dancing is your answer. Be ready for a journey that you will not regret.

Audi MPK

I started dancing Kizomba/Urbankiz in 2014. When I walked into to room, immediately I fell in love with the dance. The great energy in the room and the excitement on people faces while dancing was priceless.

The joy on two peoples faces dancing with each other especially when they have never met before, it's an amazing experience.

The benefits I have gained are huge. It has changed my life for the better. So many others and I have posted the question; what was I doing in life before the social dancing? I remember the life of going to the club to stand, drink and talk nonsense. With social dancing, it is beyond just talking and drinking, but true human communication.

For some reasons, I always want to partner dance. Once you are in it; it can feel like a drug. The art, the music, the human touch, the interaction with so many different people is worth it. I social dance for 5 hours; wake up the next day wanting to do it all over again.

Anyone with the opportunity to start dancing should do it for sure. At first, it may be different and difficult because you are learning something new. Just stick with it. You will found it joyful.

I am Audi MPK, an instructor for the dances Urbankiz and Tarraxa. I created a brand called MPK standing for Musicality, Personality, and Kizomba. Musicality is very important and something that is beautiful to watch. I felt the need to create a brand reminding dancers of Musicality.

Kizomba is a beautiful dance to millions of people around the world. Give it a try! Audi MPK

Part 2

Few Types of Social Dances and Music

Salsa

Salsa is a satisfying, playful, powerful and fun dance. Both singles and couples have a lot of social, physical and emotional benefits from salsa. The name "Salsa" means sauce in Spanish which in this context means flavor or style. Salsa dance is very sensual and flirtatious. It is a unique and creative form of self-expression.

The roots of salsa can be traced to many cultures, continents and countries, from Cuba to Puerto Rico, Colombia, Africa, Mexico and Dominica. Salsa is the product of a musical evolution of different kinds of Latin rhythms. The name "Salsa" was developed in New York. Even though it was cultivated in New York, it has a Hispanic origin. Salsa involves a mixture of Hispanic musical styles such as Són Montuno, Rumba, Guaracha, Cha-Cha-Cha, Mambo, Danzón, Guaguancó, Són, Cubop, Charanga, Guajira,

27

Cumbia, Bomba, Plena, Festejo, Merengue, etc. The individuality of many of these musical styles are still maintained while others were combined in the creation of "Salsa". It will be incorrect to give a single culture or country the credit for the creation of salsa.

You affect the chemistry of this beautiful dance with the way you move your body and interpret the rhythm of the music. There are 8 beats to every dimension of salsa music. In a basic salsa step you're required to move on beats 1, 2, 3, stop briefly on 4, move again on 5, 6, and 7, and stop briefly on 8. Give yourself and your relationship the advantage of a new exaltation, and indulge in a perfection. Enjoy the beautiful dance which is salsa.

Bachata

It is simple and easy to learn, fast in pace, sensual in style, romantic in motion, passionate in approach and fun to dance. It is Bachata dance from the rural marginal neighborhood and countryside of the Dominican Republic. Bachata dance is undeniably all about hips and attitude! In becoming a well-rounded Latin dancer, the importance of Bachata dance cannot be overemphasized.

Bachata is an outgrowth and a close relation of the pan Latin-American romantic style known as Bolero. Over the years, merengue (a danceable and fast paced music also from the same country) has influenced it. This passionate, suave form of dance is immensely popular throughout Latin America and across the western world.

Newcomers will find Bachata relatively easy to learn, dance masters will equally have a great deal of freedom to show off their skills. Bachata dance teaches you to become more in touch with yourself and be free. More than you can with other Latin dances, you can on a more personal level, connect with your dance partner.

Merengue

The merengue is the national dance of its country of origin; the Dominican Republic and also happen to be the most popular Latin American dance that hold much national importance to the country. Merengue is a fun dance that is quite easy to learn. It is well suited to the small, crowded dance floor.

Merengue dance is a fusion of African and European cultures that quickly became a force to reckon with because of its simple movements and steps. Dance partners could hold hands all through the dance or detach while still in close contact.

The word "merengue" is the Spanish alternative of the French word "meringue" which means "a confection produced from sugar and beaten egg whites". The description fit the "fluffy and light nature of the dance where dancers shifts their weight gradually between their feet in a very fluid motion" and is also applicable to the dancers' frothy and sweet character.

Merengue is arguably one of the easiest Latin dances to learn. The rhythm is constant and the beat clear. Just like Bachata which is another famous Dominican dance, the priority is on simplicity in step patterns instead of style and drama. Dancers make few turns if any. When turns are made, they are casual walking steps instead of the spin turns that is synonymous with Salsa.

Kizomba

It's no longer news that Kizomba social dance like a wildfire is taking over the world. It's the rave of the moment in the dance world. It's giving dancing styles like salsa, cha-cha, merengue and Bachata a run for their money. Because of its characteristic beat, you can dance it to nearly all music. The hip-swinging moves of Kizomba is sensual and slow unlike the fast-moving dances that is popular in Latin cultures. It's a sensual dance that provides you with maximum freedom of expression.

The word "Kizomba" is Angolan and it means "party". Kizomba was developed in Angola in the 1980s. This dance style is strongly derived from Zouk. Zouk found its way to Angola, where it combined with Semba (the Angolan root of Brazilian samba) and traditional Angolan music, resulting in Kizomba. The word "Zouk" is a French word for "party" or "festival".

The strong attraction to Kizomba is as a result of its beats and sensuality. Kizomba has come on the scene as a more modern dancing style with its sensual beats and catchy music. It speaks more to our times than Bachata or salsa.

Kuduro/ Afro-house

This is not a partner dance but worth knowing. If you've been to any of the clubs in the major metropolitan cities, odds are that you've danced to the vibrant, pulsating, and infectious Kuduro dance. Kuduro is a highly energetic and unique dance. It's inspired by a lot of things in the environment, in our world. A Kuduro move could be any kind of move. For instance, we could imitate a frog's movement, the marching of soldiers, or the movement of animals. Everything and anything could make a movement."

Kuduro was born during the late 1980s in the streets of Luanda, the capital of the West African country of Angola. This dance began with young musicians who started fusing African percussion samples with "soca" rhythms and simple calypso to develop a music style then known as "batida." It's the uncompromising, raw sound of the streets of Angola.

The word "Kuduro" means 'hard ass', 'in a hard place' or 'in hard times', to show what the country has gone through and still goes through. It mixes traditional Angolan Zouk, Semba and Kilapanga with Western house and techno.

With Kuduro you feel free, alive and ready to conquer the world. The beat is fast, raw and insanely honest. It's the people's choice. This explains the reason for the high popularity in its home country and a lot of other countries. Kuduro is conquering the world.

Kuduro is telling you to take a break from your life's struggles, pains and disappointments and enjoy music, dance and set your mind free. This dance is from the streets. From the mind to your heart and feet. It's preaching a positive message.

A message of hope, inner strength and indomitability.

Tango

Tango is a playful, understanding, conversational, sensitive and respectful dance between two people. It is not lacking when it comes to very rich potential for connection, expression and improvisation, and is danced in both traditional and modern styles. As a result of the dance's history, the close connection between dancing partners and the character of the music, it's often referred to as a passionate dance. Tango is sharing a moment of understanding, trust and intimacy with another individual. When you tango, there is no worries, no past, no future, and no pain, just you and your partner, saying to the music "come take over". It's pure magic.

The history of Tango is not only complex but also fascinating. It is a sensual ballroom dance birthed in the 1880s on the shores of the Rio de la Plata which happens to be the border between Uruguay and Argentina. Tango has since come to be known as one of the most spellbinding of all dances.

The Argentine tango is filled with the desire to listen to, converse with and understand your dance partner. When compared to modern tango, the Argentine tango is much more affectionate and personal. It's a collaborative dance that encourages the building of trust, sensitivity and respect between partners.

Zouk

Zouk is a fun, modern dance suitable for all ages. For many in the younger dance crowd, Zouk has rekindled an interest in partner dancing. For those who have experience dancing other traditional Latin dances (and even West Coast Swing), many of the moves, techniques or concepts from those dances can be imported to Zouk, making it relatively easy to adapt to this dance.

In addition, Zouk can be danced to a variety of music and a variety of moods, making it a versatile dance to know. This sensual and energetic dance has roots in Brazilian Lambada and Samba, while the music has French Caribbean roots. Zouk has a characteristic wave-like movement, elongated steps and striking hair movements by the lady. The movements are a rhythmic side to side and a rippling forward and back wave-like motion. Like many dance styles, Zouk is ever evolving. There are a few different lines or styles of Zouk, the main three derivations at the moment (April 2015) being 'lambazouk', 'traditional zouk' and 'modern zouk'

Level of Dancers

Beginner Dancers

Beginner dancers are fairly new to a particular dance, and they predominantly use their mind while dancing. Their main focus is to get the steps right, so they think a lot while conducting the steps. This is completely normal because they are applying the fundamentals that they learned. Without applying the fundamentals into practice, they will easily forget the steps. An active memory is needed at this stage. Beginners use memory tricks to recall the moves learned in class. They are not familiar with the dance. It is mostly a struggle to pass this stage. It takes a lot of courage and practice to master the fundamentals.

If you are a beginner dancer, you should understand that this is a great place to be, all great dancers started here. Without the basics, there will be no foundations.

It is like, in writing, there are no words without alphabets. With alphabets, you can construct into words and into sentences. But as for a child learning the alphabets seems very hard but it is possible though. You work your way form the symbols of alphabets, to words and finally to full sentences, and to point that you can use proverbs, idioms to express your thoughts. With this mastery of the language, you don't have to think to call a pen, "a pen". You just say it as you see it.

At beginner's level, you have the opportunity to learn something new that is practical. And it feels amazing to learn practical things.

Don't worry too much about trying to master the basics right away, be with the journey, and focus on the experience. Have fun when in class and out for socials. Practice as needed and one day, not far away you will see your dance skills at intermediate levels. You'll begin to wonder how quickly you got there just like a student that suddenly realized the mastery of the alphabets and words simultaneously. I call it realization because is something, you, yourself know, it is a deep feeling and understanding of the fundamental. Once you get it, the knowledge is acquired. It is not like learning and memorizing patterns with a group for performance. It's a deeper knowledge of the basic, at this point you should be able to analyze it, break it down, and lead the fundamentals effortlessly.

Intermediate Dancers

An Intermediate dancer is the one who passes the beginners level and predominantly uses their mind and body while dancing. They master the fundamentals but yet not at advanced level. Their main focus is to connect the dots. They spend a lot of time learning how to transition from one move to another. I call this stage the 'conjunction stage' because this is the stage that can connect you to advance level. You use alphabet and words that you learn at beginners level into sentences. This is the stage where you are prone to hit the wall because you do a lot of thinking simultaneously with your body movements. And it can be very discouraging when you hit the wall; it feels like there is no way out. Some people tend to stay at this level for a long time because of the wall, and they get comfortable and won't challenge themselves more.

One day, on our way coming from Atlanta Kizomba congress, I had a great conversation with Mike Ahombi, an Urban Kizomba dancer, while in the car driving back to Charlotte, he told me that "when you find yourself at the wall of confusion or darkness, think of it like a house. You are on the corner of it even if you can't see, if you keep knocking on the wall all the way around, there will be a point, where you will find a door to exit or a window to exit. " in other words, if your goal is to reach an advanced stage, you have to be persistent in your learning and never give up to the wall of darkness.

Your mind and your body need to works well together in other to go beyond this stage. For example, when you learn a move or pattern and of course these moves can be traced to basic steps, you will have to recall those moves and apply it when dancing. Just remembering the moves won't help, the application of the moves correctly is vital. You will spend a lot of time recalling and applying steps. And this can be a challenge because when dancing with a partner, you have a fraction of second to transition from one move to another or one basic step to another. Connecting the dots can be very difficult especially when musicality and timing are involved. That is why you spend half of your time learning the moves and the rest on musicality classes. Here you will learn how to transition on time, half time and even against the time. Intermediate and beginners are the majority on the dance floor. Most dancers stay on this level because it takes more commitment to be at advance level.

Advanced Dancers

You are an advanced dancer when you have gone through fundamentals steps and intermediate step successfully. You learn to use mind, body, and spirit simultaneously while dancing. It is not about just dancing, it is about feeling the music, making it beautiful. You are an advanced dancer when you can internalize the music and interpret it into movements without distorting the fundamentals of the dance. At this level, you can use complex sentences and idiomatic expressions to express yourself. As you dance, people watching you are drawn to your movements because you dance with your whole being. You are fully present, your movement is clear and your soul is fully involved with it.

Enjoyment and making it beautiful is their main focus while dancing. They spend a lot of time on embellishment and beautiful styles. Through this, they develop their own personalities and styles that are unique to them. This helps them stand out from the crowd. Advanced dancers are the master of the dance. They are the one who has gone through thousands of hours, taking classes at all level. They have gone through basic and intermediate steps learning and practicing for long hours.

These dancers are the one who can help you with your dance goals. Because of their experiences they can give you constructive criticism on your dance moves. They can help you polish your movements, your posture, leading, musicality and many more. Hint for beginners. Always befriend an advanced dancer; it will increase your learning speed.

These dancers eventually become instructors and professionals performers. Advanced dancers are not the majority on the dance floor. Hence many dancers are not up for the commitment involved with it. Once you reach this level, you become fully expressive, you feel more like an artist. With the floor, like canvas, you may paint the way you feel, the way you like it. This is the level where you are free to break the rules; the rules that you have learned at beginner level. You can break it without distorting the fundamentals of the dance. People, who love and appreciate art, can see your uniqueness and appreciate it.

Once you reach this level, learn to share, a treasure has no worth if you are buried with it.

Followers (Follow) and Leaders (Lead) In Social Dancing

Before you start any partner dance, it is important to know some of the rules and role play. In terms of roles, whether you are a man or woman, you may choose to lead or follow. Or sometimes do both.

Followers: In social dancing, followers as the name implies, follows the leads. Followers can be female or male. As a default, ladies are usually followers and men are leaders. It is important to understand that most partner dance such as salsa, Kizomba, followers' initiates' step beginning with right foot. In my classes as a memory trick, I always said this joke that. "Ladies are always right "of course guys, this is up to an endless debate.

Leaders: These dancers are the one leading the followers. They are commonly men as default. Leaders are the one who initiates most of the moves. It is important to understand that most partner dance such as salsa, Kizomba, leaders mostly initiate steps beginning with their left foot. Leaders are the one who supposed to take initiative to ask a follower for a dance.

Part 3

How to Find Dance Classes and Events

Facebook

Facebook is a great platform in dance communities. Many dancers and instructors use the platform to their advantages. You also may use this social media platform to stay connected with a particular dance group, instructors, and classes in an area. For example, keywords such as Charlotte Latin dance, New York salsa dance, Paris Kizomba, can help you find the active groups and instructors in that particular area. Once you found your preference, stay connected by hitting the like button on the page or joins the group. By liking the dance group page, you are automatically connected to their classes' schedules and events information. Dance festival also uses this platform to post about the upcoming events. Almost all dance festival post their event on Facebook. To find a festival on Facebook, use keywords search to find it. For example, if you're into Kizomba dance, keywords such Miami Kizomba festival will bring you the dates and events details.

Facebook is also a great tool for connecting with the friends that you have met at classes and events. Sometimes it's hard to manage many contacts on your phone. This site allows you to easily communicate and stay up-to-date with them.

Since it is a great platform for pictures and videos; dance festivals and instructors usually post pictures & videos on their page from the previous events and classes. You can use those pictures as a souvenir and the video to refresh your memory. Warning: the Facebook platform can be so addictive, use it wisely. If you do not prefer Facebook other platforms are available to you to accomplish similar goals of staying connected.

Instagram

Personally, I use Instagram for videos. It's a great platform for videos without dealing with all the unnecessary feedback on Facebook. I use this platform to post a lot of videos from my classes and some pictures too. With Instagram, you can easily find dance videos with a hashtag search option, for example, #Bachata, #Tango, #Kizomba will bring you results of the related tags. If you want to engage in social media without dealing with too much information, Instagram may help. Many dance studios, instructors, festivals have an Instagram page. By simply following someone or group, you get connected with them.

Like Facebook Instagram also allows users to communicate with each other through instant messenger services for free. Some of your friends will have both Facebook and Instagram or at least use one of these platforms.

If social media is not a preference for whatever reasons here are some platforms you can use to your advantage.

Groupon

Groupon platform is a great source of getting discount on dance classes. Established dance companies have great deals on Groupon. For example, dance studios can have a discount on six weeks dance classes or ten classes for an affordable price. Once you buy the voucher, you can take these vouchers to class and redeem it in exchange for the service. These businesses on Groupon are legit and registered with the state.

Because Groupon let customers rate businesses, you have the advantage to check the quality of their services before buying. Simply read through the comments and feedback from the previous students. These comments kind of give you an understanding of the services you are getting.

These discounts can be helpful. If you want to save money on dance class and support local businesses Groupon is a great option.

Meetup

On meetup, you can find and join a dance group with the intention of meeting the group members in real life. You are guaranteed to meet members at their scheduled meeting date. This could be in a form of meet & greet, parties, events or even classes and workshops. Meetup has communities' mindset. According to their website, "Meetup brings people together to create thriving communities" On meetup, you don't have to worry about constant notification on your smartphones, such as the ones you get on other platforms like Facebook.

Meetup is a great option to join a group with a specific set of Interest such as dancing, singing, and hiking. The group leaders usually post events and classes that you can attend.

It is important to read the descriptions about the group and know what it is about before joining.

Furthermore, once you join the group, before attending the meetup check to see if the events are free or a paid one. Some organizer charges for attending the event and it might not be to your knowledge. Be prepared and ask questions when in doubt. Add meet up to your list if you are not into social media bells and whistles.

Eventbrite

Eventbrite is designed to promote and sell tickets for the upcoming event such as music festivals, marathons, workshops and many more. According to the website, their mission is "To bring the world together through live experiences".

One of the great features about Eventbrite is the ability to search with keywords and purchase tickets in the same platform. These keyword inquiries can bring you results on related search. If you're interested in salsa dance, with a keyword search "salsa", you can see results of salsa event in that particular area. Dance socials, classes, and festivals use Eventbrite and Facebook together. These organizers post event on Facebook and Eventbrite attaching a link to purchase the tickets on Eventbrite' and sometimes with a different ticketing or processing company such as ticket-leap. Consider Eventbrite if you want to buy your ticket right away and skip social media.

Google Search

As you may know by now, the term "Google it" has become very popular. It is popular for reasons. Google search engine can be a very effective tool to inquire about a wide variety of topics. I use Google to search for a specific dance.

With a keyword search on Bachata dance, you will find the result on texts and videos on YouTube. You can get a visual look at the dance before committing to a class. Since the platform is available to anyone with a free account. The dance videos and the quality on YouTube solely depend on the individual who may have posted it. When in doubt about a specific dance, pick a phone and call a local dance instructor for further clarifications.

Google search is a great tool to get information about a dance company, classes, festival, and event anonymously.

Well established dance schools own a website where can find all the details about their specialties, instructors, and obtain contact information.

With a website link from Google, you can read about the dance instructors, their biography. Detailed information such as, what to wear and class schedules can be found on the website.

Most dance festivals have their own website. You can learn about instructors, performers, scheduled during the dance festivals. Keep YouTube as your friend to keep up with your favorite dance instructors, most of the instructors have a YouTube account to post latest dance videos from the workshops.

Part 4

What Shoe To Wear?

As for any skills, there are tools designs to help you perform well. One of the important tools to add in your dance toolbox is a great pair of dance shoe. Beginner dancers always want to know about what kind of shoe to wear. I usually get this question a lot. "I signed up for your class, what shoe should I wear'? This depends on what type of dance you are interested in, and your gender.

Latin Dance Shoe

For ladies with interest in Latin Dance such as (Salsa, Bachata, Samba, Cha-cha-cha, Rumba, Paso Doble, and Jive) Latin dance shoe will do it. Ladies typically wear open-toed shoes with a flared heel. As for beginners, it is recommended to start with two-three Inches heel with a flared heel. The flared heel provides stability and support.

Above three inches it is not advisable unless you are a proficient dancer on heels. However, you may gradually add half an inch increment in time, if you desire. For example, you may add half of an inch to two inches, to gain two & a half inches.

These shoes must have non -slip suede soles for better turns and grip on the dance floor. For color wise, is up to your preference, however black is the most popular color. Light brown or flesh-colored shoes are also getting more attention, as it extends the leg line. Make sure the shoe is snug and hug fit, not too tight. If it is too tight it may cause a blister or too loose can make you trip while dancing. These shoes can be less expensive compared to ballroom shoe.

Here are examples of latin dance shoe ladies, pictures courtesy of Gfranco shoes, at www. gfrancoshoes.com. You can use coupon code "Danceshoes" for a $5.00 discount for any online purchase of a dance shoe. (As of 2018- 2019)

GFranco Shoes

Ballroom - Standard dances for

ladies (Waltz, Viennese Waltz, Foxtrot, and Quickstep)

These Dance shoes are designed to have tin soles which allow you to glides on the dance floor with the good amount of grip. This shoe should look nice, be comfortable, and provide protection, designed for performance and support posture.

Shoe types vary based on the dance listed above. In standard dances, your posture is an essential part of the dance. Mostly dancers use closed toe pumps for standard and open toe shoes for Latin dances. Some typical dance shoe to consider purchasing is open-toe, closed toe, pumps. The heels usually range from one- three inches and can be flared or stilettoed. If you are new into ballroom dancing, try to get a shoe that is closed- toe pump with two - two & a half inches, with a flared heel and make sure it has an ankle strap. This will pass for ballroom dancing. As always it must be non-slip suede sole for better grip and slides while dancing. Some ladies prefer closed shoe because it provides better protection against being step-on while dancing and it also protects your toenails. Most standard dance heel is position in the center, under the foot. This helps the backward movement.

Stiletto heel

These are slim, long pointed heel usually for ladies. This type of heel can add great style to your looks. However, these heels are typically for experienced dancers. The slim structure of it does not support proper balance and stabilization compared to the flared heel, whereas the flare shape heels at the end is designed to support your balance.

As an add-on, you can also buy a clear flare heel cap to your Stiletto heel for better stabilization on the floor. The clear form of it will be barely noticeable. Before you invest in a stiletto shoe, make sure you are extremely comfortable with dancing with high heels. Beginner, are advice to start with flare heel.

Strappy-Sandal

These sandals are super lightweight dance shoe with up to three inch heel. These sandals are a great option for outdoor dancing in the summer. When choosing a sandal, for better contact on the dance floor, make sure your toe is close as possible to the front edge of the shoe. You may find some ladies prefer their toes to hang over the shoe front edge so that they can feel, point their foot to the floor more easily. The shoe companies have varieties of the style, heel, looks you choose from.

Pumps Shoes

Other types of shoe are the Pumps. They are another design found in the Latin dance for ladies. Pumps shoe has an opening along the side of the feet with a closed toe box. It is also secured with an ankle strap.

Latin Dance Shoe for Men

Men usually buy dance shoes when they want to take dancing more seriously or want to join a dance competition. That said, try to invest in a good dance shoe, the material on it is designed to enhance your dancing and even prevent knee injuries. Most common Latin dance shoes for men are the "Cuban" heels, about one and half inches heels. Typically lighted weighted, flexible and Oxford in shape.

The most common color is black and white or two-tone color mixed. Make sure it's all non- slip suede sole. There are different choices to choose from, Patent leather, nubuck or leather, whichever you choose must fit well, hug and snug like fit. However, if you just want to try out dancing and see if you like it or not, to save money; you may buy a stick-on suede sole for one of your nice shoes at home. By simply attaching the stick on suede soles at the bottom of your shoe, this can turn your ordinary loafer into a semi-dance shoe. These soles are inexpensive, a great way to get you started quickly without a lot of investment on the shoe. However, buying an official dance shoe is a better investment for the long run, especial for Latin dancers.

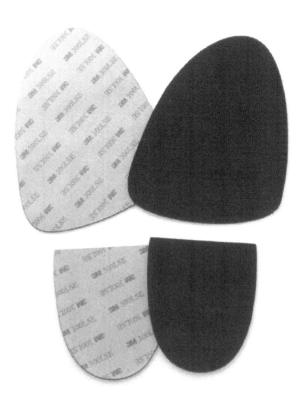

Some things to consider when buying a dance shoe

For beginners, buy your first shoe in person, from a local dance shoe store, sometimes you may need to travel to a major city nearby to find such store. You can also buy it from a dance festival event. These festivals usually have shoe vendors. Once there, an experienced salesperson should be able to help you. This will help you know the correct size and type that you may need to get next time online. If you don't know where to buy locally, ask your local dance instructor or research online for a nearby shoe store, the shoe that you choose must fit well is snug-fit, hug-fit, but not too tight to cause discomfort. Try many types before purchasing it. Keep in mind, the shoe has to be comfortable and functional

Rubber sneaker soles are not a good fit, especially for Latin and ballroom dances. It can stick to the floor and cause knee injuries. Even leather soles can be dangerous too because they can slide too much that may lead you to trip.

Buy a dance shoe that has tin suede soles, with a steel shank for support. Overall it must be lightweight and super flexible.

In addition, for efficiency, you may buy a pair of insoles for your dance shoe. These insoles are very comfortable and it increases the numbers of hours you can take on the floor. I highly recommend this for dance festivals. Buy the insoles that are for runners shoes. Don't get the "gel" types of insoles. They can be too heavy to feel the floor.

For ladies, if high heel hurt tries and arch for support. If you can purchase only one type of shoes for men, it should be standard dance shoe and ladies if you can purchase only one type of shoe it should be Latin dance shoe.

Sneakers for Dancing

If you want to change your style up a little bit you can consider wearing a sneaker for dancing. These sneakers specially designed with a suede Soles for your comfort ability. These options are great for men and ladies. For men, dances such as Urban-Kizomba works best with lightweight flat soles sneakers. Consider getting a flat-sole sneaker and attached a strap-on suede sole on the bottom the shoes if needed. Or simply buy sneakers designed for Latin dance.

Practice Shoe

This is up to you. Ladies you can practice with a shoe similar to guys shoe with a higher heel or even a sneaker with suede soles. This works for guys too.

Dance Shoe Maintenance

Your dance shoe is an investment; protect it.

Most dance shoe cost for $79 -$299 that is not a cheap shoe to buy. Avoid wearing your dance shoes on the regular street, like sidewalks and streets. Dirt and cement on the street will wear it out quickly! When going to dance floor, carry it on a bag and put it on at the dance floor.

Keep your shoe polished all times, to prevent cracking apply silicon-based oil time to time. With suede sole, in time dirt will build up, you will need to brush it when it gets sticky with dirty built up.

Part 5

What To Wear/Bring

Ladies Clothing:

Once you start social dancing, Going out on many different occasion is obvious. The occasion such as social dance nights, festivals, practice sessions, pool parties will definitely be on your list to attend.

Social Dance Nights

Social dance night is a night for social dancing where partner dance music is played. Music such as Bachata, Kizomba, Salsa, Zouk, and related depending on the culture are the main music played by the DJs. Without the music and space for the dances, this night can't take place. The music is a key element to a successful social dance night. Before attending a social dance night, make sure you know what kind of music it is centered on. Some social dance nights have a focus on a particular genre, such as Bachata, and the rest is minor or not played at all. Some social dance night mix it up almost fifty-fifty, Dj will play as advertised. It could be salsa, Bachata, and Kizomba.

Occasions like these, usually ladies dress well, nice and classy. Something in between the line of Semiformal outfit will do it.

A nice stretch – flexible pant and a classy top are common. You may also wear a tight-fitting shirt with sleeves. Or even a practice skirt is fine

Just avoid tight mini-skirts, A-line skirts, or anything that may restrict the movement of the legs and thighs freely. Avoid wearing jacket and sweater while dancing; this can cause too much sweating. Only wear that jacket and sweaters when it is cold, in and out of the venue.

In summer times, it will be smart to bring extra shirt just in case you sweat more. And don't you forget to smell pleasant!

Weekly Practice Session

These sessions are usually available in the dance community. They are designed for dancers to practice in other to become better dancers. Friend and groups usually organize these kinds of meet up. These also may apply to general classes and street dancing. Sessions like these do not require fancy or an elegant outfit.

Simple leggings and a shirt out it will pass. How- ever, the shoe you wear matters, make sure is appropriate for the floor. Do not wear a suede soles dance shoe on a concrete cemented floor. A good habit to have is to always check out your dance venue before going out. You can easily Google search the location or ask someone about the venue. And don't you forget to smell pleasant!

Pool Parties

This one can be very fun. Pool parties are mainly found at the dance festivals or dance congress. They serve as an intermission session between the classes and the social dance night.

What to wear? It is obvious, dress like you are going to a pool party! Ladies wear that favorite bikini Swimsuit, show that body, and feel comfortable with your body.

Men's Clothing:
Social Dance Night

A business casual will be pleasing. Or you may even mix up with a business outfit and casual outfit. For example, you may wear a business long or short sleeve T-shirt with a casual pant. It is a lot easier for men. If you have dress black pant and a colored pant, you can alternate between those pants with a nice shirt. Your regular suit and jacket might not be a good option. But you may go for a light blazer for more business look.

Since there will be a physical connection between you and your partner. Avoid wearing shorts unless it for practice session and pool parties. It will be smart to bring an extra shirt just in case you sweat more.

Generally, dancing is a physical activity and there is a need to dress for the occasion. Your dress must be fashionable and functional, it must support your movements comfortably. Finally it is of upmost importance to smell pleasant!

Hair and Nails and Others

Hair needs to be kept neat and tidy. Long hairs that are not shortened or tied up in a ponytail can be a nice weapon for slapping your partner. Consider ponytails or tie your hair back nicely or find a method that will work for you and your partner. Any hairstyles that will not be a dangerous distraction to you and your partner are welcome. A loose hair can easily be entangled on guys' shirt cuff button. Or it can be entangled with bracelet, which can be very painful. Imagine your hair getting a trapped on a bracelet while initiating a turn. Pulling your hair back can help clear your view while dancing. Sometimes certain moves require your full engagement and if you can see your partner suggestions it will help the more. Any hair accessories should be firmly attached to the hair properly.

Things to avoid wearing on the dance floor Open, loose bracelets, watches, some bracelet and watches are easy grips on hair while on turns moves. It may pull off hairs, when entangles that can turn the joy moment into unpleasant moment.

Nails: Make sure nails are short to avoid scratches on somebody face.

And if you have to wear glasses make sure it is not loose. Just be aware that they can fall on the dance floor and someone might step on it. Mainly, just be mindful of other people you are going to dance with.

Classy Dancer

Classy is simply being clean, cool and gentle in and out. It manifests in the way you speak to people, dress, and dance. Classy is the definition of a great dancer who dances to share the joy with every partner he or she dances with. Be classy on the dance floor because you will stand out. Consider this manner as a life style.

Great Habits To Consider In Social Dancing

Smell Pleasant

You cannot let this one slide! Remember most social dancing you will have to dance with a partner and in a dance like Bachata, Kizomba and Zouk, you will be in close embrace with your partner. It is very important to smell pleasant. Everyone wants a pleasant smell. Make sure you grab a healthy deodorant that is sweat-proof with a good mild scent. If you are going to get cologne, make sure is a mild, light scent. Too strong of a scent can be disturbing to some people, especially if you are dancing close to the person. Keep moderation into consideration.

Nice scented cologne can be a great icebreaker to start a new friendship with someone on the dance floor.

Furthermore, avoid eating food, with strong odor before going out to dance floor. Great hygiene is a must in and out if you tend to avoid great hygiene no one would want to dance with you.

However, if money is tight, just be presentable. Sometimes, you don't have to look fancy to be classy. You just have to wear a clean cloth and smell pleasant.

Smile

This change my life, just smiling I was able to gain many friend and acquaintance within few years of dancing. Your first impression is important. When you meet someone new on the dance floor, first, smile, greet them and genuinely ask their name. Write their name down so that you won't forget it later. Or use some memory tricks to remember their name. It will come handy!

If you want to really know them, you may do so by staying connected with them through Social media, or by their phone number.

Smiling doesn't require your teeth extended, although it helps. Smile from inside, and people will feel it. Just smile!

Don't forget, next time you meet the person you met before, remember their name, people like their name, is the sweetest things to here. With this simple technique, you can build up a friendship with many people.

There are few statements in these upcoming paragraphs I was reluctant to make. However, being an experienced social dancer. I have to point out few things that seem obvious but ignored sometimes. These habits are essential for your dance experience with others. It will not be a service to new and veteran dancer if I choose to omit words. This book is designed to enhance your dance experiences, and help set expectations that are simple and practical. Let's continue.

A Pleasant Breath Is Pleasing

If you smell good, people like it, and if your mouth smells good, you and the people you come in contact with would love to chat with you more. You can even have a more intimate conversation without looking the other direction because your mouth smells otherwise. The point I am saying is that your mouth must smell good. Before heading out to a dance gathering, get into the bathroom freshening up. Brush your teeth.

On your way to a social, stop by the local convenience store and grab a mouth freshener or chewing gum. This is a life enhancer for dancers. We usually dance up to four hours or more, and you are prone to bad breath, especially if you eat junk food a few hours before. This unpleasant breath can ruin the experience of your dance and the others.

Having gums with you can also save the night for someone. Often, you can even befriend someone because they ask you if you have a gum and you happen to have one. You will be surprised how many dancers you met on the dance floor that asks such question. Be a dance freshener! Carry a gum with you and share with a new and old friend as needed.

Part 6

First Time At The Social Dance Floor, New Social Dancer

Like Will Smith said, "If you going to lay a brick on the floor, even if it is one brick, make sure you lay it down perfectly well". You never know if that is going to be the last brick you ever will lay down. The same mindset should be applied while dancing with someone.

Try this...

1. Dance with an open heart, connect to your partner with the help of the music.

2. Keep a smile on your face, this is very important. I always tell my students the most important basic you will learn from me is the "smile basic". I mean genuine smile, this helps radiate great energy within and around you.

3. Keep your dance moves simple. Connect with the dance floor by dancing beautifully and gracefully. For beginners, keep your steps nice and simple. No need for advanced moves. No need to rush through the dance. Have these tips in mind, every time you go to a social dancing,

someone is going to compliment you for paying great attention to them.

Be a great dancer with basics and tap into your why?

Great dancers dance from the heart, not tricks or bunch of embellishing moves. Of courses, those tricks can make your dance look great at a competition with dancing with the stars. Most of the time, there is limited space to do those tricks. The truth is that, at the social dancing floor, many dancers are not professionals. They are their just to have fun with few basic moves with connections. As for beginners, I know it can be intimidating to get started on social dancing. I know you don't want to look incompetent. Often, I have some student who refuses to come to the social until they feel like they feel comfortable. However this does not have to be the case for you. Actually to become a better dancer, whatever few basic moves you learn from the class, the most beneficial next step is to go apply it on the social dance floor. Always remember when you go to the social dance floor, you will always find someone at your level. Beside all the dancers at the floor, were not born with that dance skills. They had to learn it from basic steps to more advanced steps. In other for you to get better in dancing, you must apply those skills you learn from classes to the actual social settings comfortably. The more you put yourself on the floor, the better you will become. There is no need to be intimidated to get out there and have fun. It may be new to you, maybe a little heart pumping, yes that is actually a great thing. You are stretching yourself trying something new that has the potential to enhance your lifestyle; It definitely worth it.

The money you spent taking classes and workshops, shouldn't go wasted. Put it to work. Try to get your inspiration from the reason you started this fun journey, your big WHY?

As you proceed on social dancing, in time you will realize that it becomes easier to ask someone for a dance. You will realize that you are becoming a better dancer. You will find your own way. Most importantly you will find your unique expressions, style as Audi MPK said "your personality". This is where you will find most of the fun; dancing with your own flow to the rhythm.

Dance like you want to be there, dance like both of you are the only one that matter at the moment. Yes, because that is the truth.

Moreover, Dance with different partners to become a better leader or follower

In other to be a great dancer, you have to be able to dance with a lot of different people at a different level. This can be quite a challenge for the beginners. However, this is one of the recommended ways to become great at it. Keep in mind that every person you dance with has a different height, weight.

Some dancers, for example, leaders may find out that some ladies will need extra firmness in other to lead them effectively. And some of the ladies just a slight firmness lead can do it. Think of yourself as a chiropractor, you will need to adjust to ever partner, based on what your dance partner naturally needs. If you try to lead everyone the same way, you will probably waste energy and even cause injuries to yourself or your partner. When you dance, dance with care, adapt to your dance partner, and then learn how to adapt to your dance partner to make it easier to lead her.

How To Adjust To Your Partner?

Gradual Adaptation

Let say from a leader's point of view, the person you are about to dance with is an absolute beginner, with no understanding of the fundamentals ' Use a method I call a "gradual adaptation".

First, prep her by starting with a basic step for warm up, if she responds well to that; next, add few more basic steps, then advance basics moves. You can see this unfolding pattern. By using a gradual process, you can adapt to her level of dancing, without making her dance for you, but dancing with her.

What if she fails to respond well to your leads, and other moves? Then keep it simple and stick to the basics and be patient with her. Because First-timers can easily get frustrated and they might give up if they encounter self-consumed dancer.

You don't need to master the Fundamentals in other have fun at a dance social.

Sometimes it can be difficult for a new dancer to adjust to social dancing because they are not familiar with the steps. The most common excuse I hear from a new dancer is that "I am not good at it yet, so I don't want to mess it up at the socials" it is true that you are new to the culture; waiting until you feel great at it, won't help much for your experiences.

The excuses come here when you saw other advanced dancers doing a lot of different patterns simultaneously, you are prone to get intimidated by it and you may start comparing yourself and making a calculation. Calculation such as how long will it take me to get at this level? This can be a source of inspiration or discouragement.

This is perfectly normal, you don't have to compare yourself to the professional dancer, and all you need to do is to participate to the best of your abilities. The few moves that you master can take you through one song. Next time you find yourself on a dance floor, just get involved with it. Deliver what you know. With consistency, you will be an advanced dancer and someone will enjoy watching you express yourself.

Guide For Couple On Social Dancing

Dance date

Social dancing is a fun place for a date, especially for first date, since both partners getting to know each other. Due to the physical nature of dancing, it allows partners to loosen up in an environment that is relaxing and interactive. This environment allows you to give a little bit space to your partner without being clingy or needy. You may use this time to dance with other dancers back and forth. This also allows you and your partner the opportunities to have a great time. Verbal conversation is limited here hence is a physical game. The main conversation is body language. This makes it different from the traditional dinner date.

For the first-timers, try to catch the introductory or beginning class before the social dance night starts. This brief intro class is usually about fifteen minutes - thirty minutes class is to help new dancers to get familiar with the basics. Almost most dance socials have this quick introductory class. Just make sure you arrive on time because they are brief class. This way you might learn new basics steps.

Ladies, please don't get salty if your man dances with another woman and the same for men too.

If you know you are the jealous type or clingy type, it is best not to take your partner to a group dance class or social dance night. The fact is that, in a group class or social dance night. You got to understand that we dancers dance in a rotational base system I call it the "Dance wheel"; this helps people with or without a partner guaranteed dance. The rotation is there to balance out the movement of event. And thus it creates an altruistic space. We dance to create joy and share the joy with everyone in the room.

That is why, in my class, which is designed for couples, even though most of the students come with their partner. I make sure every student rotate to a new partner until they get back to their respective partner. In other words, every student who is present during the class will have the chance to dance with each other. This help to set the stage for new dancer about sharing culture.

Yes, it is true that sharing is caring. It is important we are in it together, not everybody has a dance partner on the dance floor. In fact, this is a big challenge to obtain and maintain balance in any dance. Sometimes there are more ladies and sometimes the opposite.

Note that the more you dance with different dancers the better you become. It is okay if your partner asks someone to dance with them, be a happy dancer and gladly accept the invitation. Sometimes being too clingy to your partner on a date can be a turn-off. Letting go and come back to you is attractive.

Tips that work for me

When I take a date on a dance social, like salsa or Kizomba dance party; I acknowledge her by dancing two to three songs back to back with her. That way, when I start dancing with other dancers she won't feel left out. Next, I always keep a mental note to come back to her after every thirty min to dance a couple of songs together again. I keep this back and forth going to keep maintaining a balance and she will never be left out.

There is always another dancer who will be dancing with your partner. And you will be dancing with other partners. This back and for will keep the floor balance and interactive, as long as you always come to back original partner. This will make a fun interesting date you both you. If the social or the dance festival happen or have a special performance, you may use that special occasion to get close to your partner and enjoy the show together, after the performance takes pictures as a souvenir.

Part 7

How To Ask Someone To Dance With You: Ladies And Gentleman

Art Of Confidence, Invitation, Consideration, and Smile

Asking some to dance with you is a simple skill that can be mastered. This is an art of confidence with invitation, consideration, and smile. There is no one general rule. You need to have the courage to approach the person with some confidence. No need to be overly confident but be yourself. Since most people on the social dance floor are there to dance, it is easy to get many dances almost effortlessly. The expectation is already set. All you have to do is to play by the rules. It is important to understand that in a social dance culture, we do not reject a dance invitation from someone. Unless you have to for some valid reasons to not dance with that person; and you do so as politely as possible. That being said, if any dancer blatantly snubs your invitation for prejudice reason and then go on to dance with another person, please report it to the event organizer .If this is a habit by the dancer, there should be some preventive measures done by the organizers of the events. There should be a social media BOLO list (be on lookout) in the social dance communities for prejudice dancers. This should mitigate such behaviors in social dancing world.

Before you approach a dancer, make sure the person is available or be close to the dancer until he or she is available. If the person is tired sitting down and taking off her shoe, this might not be a better time to approach her. Consider all available options in other to minimize rejection.

For guys, hunting is in our nature, so you got to use it here. Don't approach her like a hungry tiger though, she might just run away for good. If she is busy dancing with another person that is probably not the right moment to ask her for a dance. Wait until she is free or ask any lady who is available at that moment. The secret of being successful in getting someone to dance with you lies on your consideration or timing.

For example, when you see an available lady that you want to invite her for a dance, gently go for it, approach her with a smile. Then extend your hand for a dance. And simply say 'let's dance' with you hand extended plus a smile on your face. She will attend to your suggestion.

Of course most people on the dance floor are in social-mode. There is no need to worry about rejection, if it happens, handle it gracefully and move on to the next partner. There is nothing to lose. There are always people available to dance with you, no matter what level you are.

To increase your chances of success try this method.

Invitation: Invite her to dance with you. Approach her with confidence, not cockiness

Smile: With a smile, extend your right hand and say this" "shall we dance or let's dance"? You can use the word "dance" even in a foreign county to invite someone to dance with you. At times, words are not even necessary. They can be a waste of time; you may drop it and go directly with body language suggestion. And still be successful at it. Highly likely, she will accept the invitation. Remember ladies like for a man to take charge especially at the right moment. Don't just sit on the dance floor watching people. Get in there, have fun with many dancers as possible. If a lady rejects your extended hands, no need to make a big deal about it. It could be a lot of different reasons. Just simply move on to the next one.

Most of the times, on the dance floor, you will have more ladies than men. This imbalance happens a lot. Men are in high demand at times. You will likely not get rejection like you may have at the local tradition clubs.

Guys try to be a gentleman, if a lady approaches you and ask for a dance, you should try not to reject the offer at all; because it takes a lot of effort for a lady to ask a man for a dance. This is not a men strip club, where you let the lady serve you a dance. Here we have to take the initiative and keep it rolling evenly with many dancers as possible.

As for ladies, the common tradition is to wait for a man to ask you to dance. This is not a set rule. It is just seeing to more attractive for a man approach you for a dance. Just like men supposed to hunt, provide and protect the family. This is a very admirable feature in partner dancing, a tradition that has been kept. Play your roles considerably.

However, it is not a fixed rule that ladies can't ask for a dance. You just have to use your intuition. Sometimes a man is available and he is probably a new dancer. You might have to lead him to initiate the first step.

Moreover, some ladies are big on dancing with their favorite dancers. They will line up just to dance with him. Guys also like to be approached considerably.

It is perfectly okay to wait until he is free to ask him to dance with you, as long as you approach him when he's available. Do so with a smile too, we welcome this approach. Just don't think he owes you a dance. If he didn't ask you for a dance, especially when both of you were available, don't fret about it, because another guy will ask you for a dance.

Here are some of the reasons you may not be invited by a dancer

Social Dancing is a game between two individuals. And it keeps on going between individuals endlessly. Looking from a far distance across the room, this interaction can look a little bit chaotic. Every dancer is dancing uniquely in their own ways to the same music creating a beautiful electron. Once you are in the middle of it; you easily get lost in the midst of it. Time seems like a moment to moment.

Whenever there are a man and a woman in the setting, there is some kind of a gameplay between each partner. There is a cause and effect which I find interesting, that a man and a woman are both players in this game of seductions. We are in this one together. The dancers might not pay attention to you for different reasons but here are some common reasons.

Ladies, The Reasons He Did Not Invite You For A Dance

More Ladies than Men:

This is common all around the dance community, usually; there are more ladies available to dance than men. This is partly because ladies are more proactive in activities like dancing especially in the western cultures. Ladies are the one taking this dance workout classes, taking their men to dance class dates. The North American men culture is full of, American football, basketball, baseball and many more. Growing young boys are not encouraged to take dance class compare to girls. For example, when you visit South America such as Columbia they have social dance festival in every major city throughout the year. Kids, boys, and girls learn to dance different social dance styles at early age. Most of them grow up to love and continue dancing throughout their life.

In my dance classes, I often hear from my female students that I had to drag him here to take this lesson. What makes me feel happier is after the class, the men tend to enjoy the class. It is not that the men don't enjoy social dancing. It is just a cultural difference. The more expose men are to social dancing the more they will be open up to it. Ladies, if you have guy friends, you can help increase men numbers. Introduce them to the social dancing culture. If the men know ladies are going to be there, of course, men will be there.

You Scare Him Off.

Ladies if you aren't in a good mood. Please just don't make it to the dance floor. Or have a glass of wine or something to help you relax. At a social setting, you got to know that, you are going to socialize with people. The best way to miss the dance is to have an attitude with your partner. With a nasty attitude around you, he will sense it right away. How does the guy know? Your facial expression can reveal your mood easily. Moreover, guys can feel your presence. Your pleasant energy or unpleasant energy radiate easily to a point that the guy can sense that you are not there with him while dancing. You probably say something like this, "I can't wait for the song to finish so that

I can dance with a better dancer" Yes "you are dancing dead with him". Men get it. We just let it slide most of the time.

These manners can discourage men confident to dance with you next time, especially if he is new to the culture. To him he is trying and you are not appreciating his efforts. Even though you haven't said it, but he can feel it. If he sticks around in the dance community and become a great dancer, he probably won't consider you on the dance floor as much. Be easy with the guys; know that it takes a lot of initiatives to lead someone.

You Don't Follow His Lead But Teach

They said 'It takes two to Tango'. In other words, two bodies become one in playing roles beautifully. Basically, a guy is a leader and leads the ladies. The lady follows the leads. Both partners have to play their role, if not it becomes chaotic.

Ladies play your role to the best of your abilities. Trying to do your own thing will only create frictions. Do not back lead him unless if he asks. Sometimes beginners might not lead well, all you can do to make it an enjoyable experience for both parties. Be there with him for at least one or two songs. But if you try to lead the guy unsolicited, he might resent your suggestion for that moment. Save your energy and let him struggle for a bit. Smile about it if you can, until the song finishes. Simply tell him, "We all started as a beginner keep coming to the classes and you will get it sooner than you may think" Guys like encouraging women. In addition, recommend him to few local dance instructors.

The social dance floor is not the place to teach. It's not your job to teach him on the social floor? When beginners ask for your help, simply show him the simplest basic and have him repeat that throughout the night. He might get that basic step by the end of the social. However, it should not be your concern. The classes, workshops, pre- social classes are there for dancers to take advantage of it.

He Wants To Payback

Ladies, men's play games too. Remember how you treat the other guy on the last social when numbers were in your favor. And you decided to dance mostly with your favorite dancers. And you avoided him. He was trying to get one dance moment with you, but you were busy with your clicks.

Some guys are so sensitive and hold unfavorable emotions against you for not considering him last social event.

In return, whenever men are in demand, He played the same game you did last social. It is a payback time for him. Watch out, he might dance with all the ladies except you. So if a guy ignores you on the dance floor, reflect on it a bit. Don't worry about it though. Remember it is a game of seduction. In the end, everyone wins somehow, if you miss one dance, you will have another.

You Were Not Available To Him

This reason is very common, especially in the large socials and festivals. Must men go by "first come first have bases"? They mainly choose whoever is available to them. If you want to dance with a specific person, make yourself available by standing close to him if possible. There you will have a higher chance of getting the pick for the next dance.

The more you make yourself available to him the higher your chances are. Even the numbers are against the ladies, three to one in favor of men. You will have more dances. Be available and be visible to him, then it is not on you.

You Talk Too Much While Dancing.

This can be a complete turnoff. Meet & greet moments are greatly welcome, but it's different from being a talkative dancer.

Let say you accept a dance request from a guy, the next thing you know you are dancing with him, within few seconds of the beginning the dance, he has the window to introduce himself to you, the lady. For example, he might say "My name is Mike, and how about you"? And you replied, "Oh I'm called Jenny". You may also continue with few statements like this: In case you don't know each other "Is this your first time here"? Or "how long have you been dancing Salsa, Bachata or Kizomba"? Simple questions like this, with a quick response, can help you to break the ice. It can be accomplished within thirty seconds from the beginning of the song.

The verbal conversation is going take away from the dance. If you have to continue the conversation after the dance, do so outside of the room or at the far corner in a low tone and avoid keeping it too long. Another way to keep the conversation short and simple is to get his or her contact information after the dance, such as Facebook or Instagram, phone number to stay connected if possible.

Talking too much can take away from the dance experiences. Understand that the guy has to think before he leads; the timing of his thoughts depends on the level of his dance skill. If he is a beginner or even an advanced beginner, might miss-step while trying to lead and focus on your conversation. This will cause frictions such as stepping on your fancy shoes. Keep it simple, within the first thirty second of the dance get acquainted and move on by focusing on the art of dancing.

Men, Why A Lady Might Not Want To Dance With You

She Got Hurt While Dancing.

Sometimes miscommunication happens while dancing with your partner. The intended lead might be misinterpreted as a result you crash into each other feet or bump heads. Since most ladies dance with open toe shoe, this makes it less protective when a guy steps on her feet. This may cause marks, blemishes on the toe. These injuries can be minor or major depending on the impact. Most social dancers don't dance with cowboy boots so, most step-on will not be major. If a dancer often steps on your feet, most likely he or she might be new dancer.

To minimize injuries guys, try to lead with

clear intentions. Avoid leading too many advance moves that you are not acquainted with. Wear light proper dance shoes. With lightweight dance shoe, you are less likely to hurt your partner if you step on their feet.

Use proper posture to avoid friction. For example, leaders when dancing kizomba, instead of positioning yourself toe to toe with your partner, place your right foot in between your partner feet, and place your left foot outside to her right foot. This positioning helps creates smooth transitions as you move back and forth. And avoid stepping on her lovely toes and shoe.

Guys, You Are Probably An Ninja Dancer

Let say you are a rough rider, all you like to do is to spin her pointlessly instead of joyfully dancing with her. Keep in mind in the dance community ladies notice your moves. They are prone to communicate your patterns to their friends. Ladies have their own networking group, where members talk about interesting dancers in the dance community. They talk about things such as, how sexy a particular dancer is and how naughty a dancer is.

Dancing well doesn't mean acrobatic tricks,

at least not in the social dancing. If you don't master the moves trying to execute it can become mayhem, or even cause serious injury.

Dance with your partner heart to heart. Align two bodies into one body.

If you don't want to be rejected by ladies, keep it nice and simple with her. Dance beautifully with her. Consider safety, by helping her feel secure, that you got her on your arms. She needs to feel like you are not going to drop her in the middle of a trick. You have to be on point with you leads. Go for moves you have mastered and lay it down beautifully.

She Is A New Dancer

Some ladies will simply reject you because they are new to the dance. They don't want to mess it up, but deep down they still want to dance. All they need is a little push, encouragement from the guy. Listen to the clues.

With an invitation, she might say "I don't know how to dance" or "I don't know how to dance this type of dance" or" I am new to dance" In this situation, you have the choice to persist gently or withdraw. I prefer to persist. Try saying something like this, "welcome to the community, and let me show you few steps"

When a lady is a beginner dancer, she is more

likely to accept your invitation than a man at beginner level. Because she only has to follow your leads, if you can lead precisely well, she will enjoy the dance with you.

She Is Tired

Sometimes after dancing for few hours on those heels, she just wants to take a break for few minutes. If you find a lady sanding and probably breathing slightly faster, this might not a good time to approach her for a dance.

You Don't Smell Pleasant

I have already explained about hygiene on both sides. However, in the dance community, guys sometimes tend to ignore this more often than ladies.

Unpleasant smell can be avoidable. It's extremely important to consider proper hygiene, guys you cannot avoid this one, no way. Simply follow a basic hygiene, brush your teeth, take shower, use deodorant, wear clean clothes and smell pleasant. When in doubt, ask one of your home girls to prove to test your hygiene. That can help give you an idea what the ladies prefer in gentleman hygiene.

In social dancing, especially in festivals, you are going to come in contact with a multitude of people. You want to at least be prepared and leave a great impression with your presence. Men who smell good attract a lot of dancers. If you are single, this might help land you a butterfly on your shoulder. Take your hygiene seriously especially when going to a social dance floor.

Part 8

Ways To Be A Better Dancer

Know the Music

Music is a vibrational tool that crosses all boundaries. Music is the language and dancers are the translators. How clear your translation depends on your understanding of the music. In order to understand the music, you clearly have to listen to the music quite often. For example, if a dance choreographer wants to nail his performance. He will have to pick a song and continuously listen to the music, again and again, until he comprehends the music. He will focus these key elements of the song; elements such as high, lows, tempo, bass, claps and lyrics (if there is one) of the song. How great his performance will be, will mainly depend on how well he interprets the song through his body movements.

Mostly dance is a non-verbal communication the more you can understand the music, the better you will dance.

The dance starts with music, the song can be internal or external. Whether it is the song within you or from the loudspeaker, you will need to dance with the vibration of the wave accordingly.

Learn the language of the music and adapt to it while you are dancing. There are many of different genres composed for partner dance. Let say you are learning to dance Salsa music; you will need to learn the timing or the basics of the songs. Move on beats 1, 2, 3, stop briefly on 4, move again on 5, 6, and 7, and stop briefly on 8.

Without this understanding of the timing, it will be very hard for a dancer to comprehend the fundamentals. When both dancers got the timing right, certainly what seems very difficult become logical. Even you find yourself in the middle of Asia; you can go to the salsa clubs, lounges, and bars, to dance with a complete stranger. That is amazing, just through body language; you can bridge cultures across the globe.

In order to understand the music, it is vital to learn the pattern of the genre. Take your time to study the timing basics, tempo, and flow, of the song. That way whenever you get lost while dancing, you can always come back to the basic timing of the songs. Learning the basics of the genre will save you a lot of practicing time.

Timing or basics can be called "the rules of a dance". As a great artist once said, learn the rules like a pro, so you can break them like an artist (Pablo Picasso). As you can see it is in sequential order. You will need to tackle all these steps one by one.

Pick A Dance You Want To Learn

As I stated previously, you have to start with the music by learning all the necessary rules like timing, tempo, counting etc. Learn the genre (style) in particular; this is important because music evolve quite often. Some genre has subgenre or urban flavor. For example, Hip-hop in the 90s has evolved to Trap music in 2000s, Tango also has Tango Nuevo, Kizomba, has a sub-genre called Urban Kizomba, Bachata, has sensual Bachata. As you can see, it is important to know the specific type of genre base on your preference. Simply do a YouTube search on specific styles to help you decide or attend a dance festival for varieties of styles.

As a dance instructor and a dancer in different dances, I think; it would be smart to start learning the original form of the dance and then work your way up. For example, instead of learning the Sensual Bachata, learn the Bachata and work your way up to Sensual Bachata. The same for Kizomba start with Kizomba and gradually learn urban kizomba; because the original dance has most of the necessary foundations that you can build on.

In time you can notice the fundamental differences and similarities between both forms. With clarity in both forms, it is easy to enjoy the socials you may attend. Hence many social dance nights will mix up the old and new trending genre.

Once you can easily identify the different genres, and able to dance the basics steps effortlessly, you are a promising dancer.

How To Remember The Rules Of The Dance

Some instructors use the wording, phrases, and timing or combination of all. Phrases such as, quick- quick slow, Cha-cha-cha, side together - side together, forward and back, left & right, 1, 2,tap -1,2,tap and the list goes on.

All these memory tricks are there to help you remember the moves you may learn in class. Utilize the memory trick that works for you and use it until you master the moves.

Some dancers like counting with numbers and others prefer the phrases and wording. Numbering or counting is quite popular too; instructors use it when demonstrating a particular pattern. In dancing using memory tricks can be handy. When learning to dance

Salsa, consider counting the steps in your mind while dancing, this can be helpful for beginners. At first it might sound abnormal to count while dancing. However this is one of the quickest ways to be on beat with the song.

Whichever method you prefer, use it to your advantage. It is normal to count in your head, while dancing, especially for a beginner. You will realize that you are not making a lot of missteps if you use this memory tricks to master the moves or steps. know that the person you are dancing with, may not be a mind reader, all he or she wants only bust to have a good time with you for a moment. Understand that, it is important not to count out loud. Because if you do so, it would take away from the connection between you and your partner, unless you are practicing with your partner, then that would be okay to count out loud. If not, is best to count or use the phrase techniques silently.

Additionally, it is perfectly okay to come up with your own mental tricks in order to master the moves or the pattern or the basic steps. Sometimes coming up with your own tricks can be very useful than the conventional general tricks out there. Because it is your creation and you can refer to it in your mind quickly to the reference point.

Listen To Music

Musicality is developed not only by dancing but by listening to the music consistently enough to a point that you naturally move to the rhythm of the song. When I started social dancing, I went out to a local Cuban restaurant, to my surprise I realize that some natives are not acquainted with the common basic steps of salsa that I learned in class. However, dancing with some of them at the restaurants, I found that their rhythm was on point. They flow beautifully with their body movements. You will realize this especially when dancing with an elderly person who probably never took dance classes before, but they just know how to dance from inside-out.

It is mainly because they "learn by osmosis" These natives grew up in an environment where they constantly listened to that particular music. They naturally internalized the flow of the music. When you want to develop musicality and have great rhythm, you have to constantly listen to the music, of course with respect to practice. Be around dancers that can teach you something you don't know. Also, listen to the music to develop the rhythms, listen in your cars, showers, at the gym. Practice standing in front of your bathroom mirror, and correct out any unpleasing body movements. You don't need to have a dance partner to develop a great sense of musicality. Mimic the flow of great dances and you will finally reach a great level.

Learn Musicality

Musicality is dancing to the waves of the music; you can either ride the waves of the music or get crushed by it. In other words, musicality is simply dancing beautifully to the music; where the dancer becomes one with the music. Musicality is like making love to the music, based on the flow of the song, you can choose whichever love-making position you prefer. Just don't forget to warm up before making love. With musicality, you are bound to get lost in the music, only a person who loves and appreciates art and dance can find you.

Dancing with a partner with terrible musicality can leave you perplexed wondering what you have just tasted. But musicality starts by understanding the music and the fundamentals of the dance. Without it, it is hard to develop the musicality and can be likened to an American guy walking into a room full of Russians and he can't speak the language; It going to be difficult for him to communicate clearly.

Musicality involves hearing the music, interpreting the music and finally applying it to dance moves that you mastered. In social dancing it involves you applying your understanding of the basics or advanced moves beautifully while dancing. It also involves adding your personality to spice it up. Your personality is your identity, embellishment, flavor, swag, style. This is how you express yourself when the music gets into you.

For beginners, you don't have to master fancy tricks to be musical. All you need to know and do is simply dance beautifully to the song. If you have mastered few simple basics, just apply those ones nicely. Your partner will appreciate you taking your time and laying it down beautifully.

How To Develop Musicality

You have to start with the music, choose a genre, dance style and a song that you like, then constantly listening to the music for understanding and pay attention to the timing. This repetition will help develop the rhythm. In addition, consistently practice by yourself or with a partner to get the flow right with your body.

Learn to analyze the music, break the elements of the music for interpretation and express those elements into body movement within and out. Elements such as lyrics and melody, tempo, high and lows, pauses, Instruments, rhythm & genre, levels, textures or the feel,(how you feel the music within you in and out), the key elements to develop musicality.

When learning to dance Kizomba dance, taking few classes might help with the mechanics of the music but little with the musicality. Because musicality takes time to build. To begin, start with understanding the basics of the dance. This process will help you build a solid foundation with the mechanics of the dance, more like the rules of the dance. Then you can continue with the music, pick a song in the genre you are learning, listen to that one particular song over and over again until you are able to identify the key elements stated above.

Try this exercise, For example, pick one song and listen to it for a week. Anytime you are driving play it, gym time, play it. This repetition method will help you to master the flow of the song.

Let's begin with the instruments of the song, whether you are a musician or not, you should be able to identify the key instruments that make up the music. Some of the instruments you should easily identify are (bass, Drum, guitar, flute, bass, piano, clap) All these instruments are danceable as a one single units if you pay enough attention to it.

You may easily experiment it with Kizomba music. Focus on the bass, us it as a reference point, you will realize that the bass is constant enough to be on beat with the dance. As the base drops you can dance on the single count with the bass or double count with the base. Just dancing to the bass, you can maintain musicality.

While dancing, connect with the floor, connect with the music and connect with your partner; these connecting points serves as a proof check for musicality.

Dancing to the bass is a layer of musicality. There are many other layers available to express yourself. You may dance to the clap, lyrics, piano, cymbals, or any instruments that may be part of the song. But it is always important to find where the main rhythm lies and which instrument play the key roles in the dance. That way when you accidentally dance off beat, or against the beat, you can always come back to the flow.

Once you identify the key instruments that make the dance, you can start dancing to the entire instrument as one unit or individual unit or even back and forth between the elements. For example, you can just dance to the claps at a giving time then dance with the bass and clap at a simultaneously. Or even dance to unique pitch of lyrics in the song.

The way composers make music is thoughtful, the entire element normally complement each other as one song. This makes it easier for beginners just understanding the timing and natural dance musically. When you stick with the key instruments of the dance, such as the bass, drum. You should be okay. Other instruments are like the icing on the cake. It makes the song to come alive more.

Be curious

As the saying goes "curiosity killed the cat", however in dance word "curiosity" makes you a better dancer. Great dancers are always looking at who is doing something new, doing great at it and then copy it. In order to be a great dancer, you have to consistently take classes, be curious about the new move that you can learn, be curious about searching your moves on the internet and asking someone to help you break it down. Try and find some excitement in your new found hobby, that way you can double down on your learning process quickly. There are a lot of workshops and classes. Be proactive and take them as soon as possible. The quicker you can master the fundamentals, the more you will enjoy the dance. Make it a goal that, every week you will master one fundamental if you continue that pattern for six months. Definitely, you will easily be amazed by your progress.

Also, find friends in the dance community. Hang out with them from time to time, go to socials with them and parties. This will help build your confidence. Those friends sometimes have free practice sessions that you can take advantage of.

Be excited and curious about your new found hobby, take videos, take to time share it on your Social media pages, this might encourage your friends/followers to take up social dancing too. Collect your dance videos and see how you progress in time.

Consider Switching Your Roles

Once you master the basics, consider reversing your role for a moment. Guys are mostly considered natural leaders in the dance world and ladies followers in general. This rationale is not adopted at all times and you find ladies leading and guys following as well. That should be a common practice because in order for you to become really great at something. You have to be able to learn it and be able to unlearn it. For example, you have to be able to reverse what you learn, starting backward. If a leader actually wants to become a great leader, he or she should understand how it feels to be a follower. Whenever the dancer switches roles he can easily relate. You can easily achieve your dance goals when you can see things from the other angle. There are many female instructors out there that play both roles. Most of them are great dancers. When you can relate, you see clearly and get it.

Mainly the problem lies with guys not wanting to follow, because we feel emasculated when following with loads of complaints that don't hold water. This is understandable, however if you are really serious about taking your dancing to the next level you have to be able to differentiate between how to lead and how to follow; you have to be able to understand the other side. The quickest way to understand the other side is to experience it yourself. This can help you easily adapt to your partner.

Sometimes, guys may not have ladies available for practice; this gives you the opportunity to dance with your guy friends. You don't have to rely on the ladies all the time to practice. Step out the comfort zone to mastery.

Part 9

Types Of Dancers

A complete dance is an involvement of mind, body, and spirit. You use your mind to understand the dance. You use your body to perform the dance and you use your spirit to connect them all together with the help of your heart. It is simply like yoga but in a form of partner dance. To become a complete dancer, you must dance with your heart. This is the key to becoming a great dancer. A dance is not complete until you and your partner feel your complete involvement.

You can't dance full heartedly if you are thinking of the next thing to do right after the dance. For example, you shouldn't be thinking about the next person to dance with right after this dance or thinking about the cheesecake you left at home that you roommate might devour it before you get back home. Judging how someone is dancing next to you, can take away from the dance. With my years of experience in the dance Community, I realize that a lot of us fall into one of this category.

Fun And Party Dancers

These are the dancers who just want to have a good time. They just want to dance until they have exhausted their energy. They like to come out on Friday or Saturday night to dance to salsa, Bachata, Kizomba, Salsa, Zouk and Tango. They make good friends and dance with many people and go home to get ready for the next social. They enjoy seeing everyone on the dance floor having fun. They're people with great social skills; they don't judge but appreciate the diversity of the crowd. They are the shining lights of the dance floor. They add extra color to the dance floor. With their high energy presence, they radiate light into every dancer they come in contact with. These dancers are the one you found at the middle of dance floor leading line dance with dancers. They are all about making sure everyone has a great time of their life. Without such dancers in a festival and dance social, the event will simply lack spice.

You dancers remind us that life should be lived in a moment to moment.

Passionate Dancers

This is the kind of dancers when they mastered the art of dancing, just watching them, dance, can make you love the art. They can make you cry, happy, sad; they can even play with your emotions because they know how to passionately translate music and feelings into a body language and dance moves. Passionate dancers dance with their heart and spirit. You can feel their vibrant energy when dancing with them. They are simply in tune with dance even at beginner level. Passionate dancers see dance as life. They dance for their lifetime. It is not just a hobby but a lifetime journey. Dance is very therapeutic to them. When they are dancing, they involve their body, Mind, and Spirit, in the moments. Dance is not only a form of art but healing to their being.

These dancers are the one who takes ample of time, to take classes, workshops, private lessons. They progress steadily in their dance goal. They are not in rush to get to the top, hence they understood that it is a lifetime passion. Every year they get better and better until they reach an advanced level.

These dancers help build the dance communities. Hence they are constantly involved in the dance world. Passionate dancers pay attention to their art, they learn every possible detail of the dance. And apply it beautifully as possible. That makes them great dancers.

The dance community can't be built without these dancers; they support the growth of dance community. They are the one who talks about dance to your friend, family, and Co-workers. And take a lot of initiative to invite people to dance events. They are active dancers but are not all over the place. They maintain a good presence in the community. They dance with many people as possible when they are out in the dance socials to share they love. The dance community needs a lot of passionate dancers because you are the building block of the dance community. You attract people, dance passionately and you genuinely love people.

Love-Seekers

Love is a beautiful thing and some of us are looking for someone that we can connect with at the higher level. However, if your main reason for dancing is to seek love; you shouldn't probably start dancing. When you encounter emotional trauma/heartbreak along the way, you will give up easily on dancing. Besides, you are not guaranteed at all to find someone you will love and that will care about you also. Love relationships in social dancing are probabilities but you can be better and be an exceptional dancer if you are willing to learn that is guaranteed.

Love seekers are always going to different socials continuously until they find someone, once they do, they completely stop dancing. You will not see them until that relationship is not working anymore, and they are back on the dance floor finding another one. It's like a hungry tiger looking for food until she gets it, then when the stomach is full she is calm, and seven days later she is hungry again.

They probably don't realize that people they love may come and go but the dance always stays, the ambiance around it is always there, the fun is guaranteed, the skills you learn will stay with you forever anywhere you go, and you can use it. Dancing is a great conversation starter, if you have enough patience, you may find someone who really loves you for who you are on or off the dance floor. Then you can dance all day all night with him or her if you want to. But to place the responsibility of learning how to dance on another person unless you're a professional performer is pretty dicey.

It is smart to be on standby if you need someone in your life, however, keep your dance goals separate from it. Dance for the joy of dancing. Have no expectation but just to have fun.

Dance Police Or Judgmental Dancers

These are the ones who only approves things that suits/aligns with their sentiments. If you need mannerism class you should probably take one before joining the communities, because dance socials are known to be a fun, safe and loving place to be. We value love, passion, expression, and sharing. Being judgmental is not part of our values. Yes, it is ok to criticize some at the practice level and keep it there. Once you step into the communities, festival, social setting, you must switch from practice mode to social mode. Dance polices are the one who judge about, how someone is dancing, their styles of dancing, and their choice of clothing.

They are predominantly loud people who seek attention in many ways; being a loose lip on the social dance floor or workshops can be a turn- off. Since, you aren't the only one in the room their common expression is, "this is not the correct or right way of doing this dance", or "this is the only way you should dance" When you spend more time with them and you realize that they are always complaining about right and wrong way of doing things.

Do not fall for it, the smart thing to do as a beginner is to take many classes as possible from different instructors, there you will be able to make sense of how to dance a particular style of dance. Learn to differentiate between different styles, this helps whenever you go out for a social, whatever music comes on, you will be able to dance to it with a particular form and style without confusion. But if you take advice from those critics on the social dance floor, it can be disempowering, because most of them are driven by extreme pride. Remember that social settings are not for teaching they're there for you to enjoy the moment based on your skill level. There is no right or wrong way of expressing artistic skills, if it clicks then, you are progressing. Do your best to learn from different instructors.

Just understand that there are critics in every work of life. The best way to approach them is to rise above them. Not pay attention to the critics. Judgmental people can be very discouraging. As for a new dancer feeding on that negative energy can discourage your passion for learning to dance. Don't fall into their policing attitudes.

Show-Off Dancers

These are fun dancers as well, but rather add more flavor to the dance floor. They have too much embellishment to handle by themselves. These dancers are usually great dancers who spent many hours learning the styles and tricks; they can dance to show off in order to draw the crowd's attention to them or in order to create an impression on somebody. There could be many reasons for their fancy expression of themselves; they enjoy the art of dancing, they like to dress fancy to the social events and they feed on crowd's energy so giving them attention makes them colorful.

While it can be fun to show of your ways, keep in mind that certain outfit is not fun to dance with no matter how nice they look. Some of it might restrict your movement. An outfit such as a lady with an A-frames skirt is not ideal, and guys unless you are taller than most people a hat, fedora, maybe an obstruction to the ladies face. It is okay to show off your dance skills but when it comes to clothing just keep in mind of the functionality of the clothing. Go ahead and have fun, impress yourself and the people watching, overall it's your dance.

Watchers

These are the people who come to the dance floor just to get the feel of it. They pay the entire necessary entrance fee but really don't get involved in social dancing. They enjoying watching people perform with their styles and tricks. They enjoying going to the festival and watch professionals perform in and out. They love to dance but for some reason, they never took the first step to learn the fundamentals. For that rea- son, these people are not active in a social dancing session. It is mainly because of their lack of dance skills. They don't want to look bad on the social dance floor, so they are inactive when they come out to socialize. And they sometimes bring their friends and families just socialize for the night especially with the venue is in a bar or dance festival.

A dance floor is always in need of an active dancer whether you're a beginner or at an advanced level. We encourage people to be more active at the dance socials. Being active helps the dance wheel (rotation) continuously evenly. Especially for guys, you are always in demand to lead followers. It is okay to come and watch performances if available at the event but after the performance, it's time to put on your dancing shoes to get involved. It doesn't matter what level you are. With the understanding of one or two basics steps, you can dance all night with many dancers. People will appreciate your effort and participation. This participation can open the door to be a great dancer. It might create the longing to take dance classes to acquire a new skill that you already love but just couldn't take the first step to learn it. Most dancers are inspired by that great dancer or dancers that we watched dance beautifully. And we said to ourselves "I want to learn to do this". And we did it! If you think watching is fun, try participating, just try and involve yourself in dancing. The dance world is full of expression, Joy, art, love, romance, and beauty. The next time you are on the dance floor be more active than usual try to dance with many people as possible.

Part 10

Habits To Be Avoided

Don't Be A Creep!

Social dancing settings are safe and a loving place to be. This conducive atmosphere is a beautiful tradition that has been handed down from one generation to another. The social dancing culture encourages courtesy in all deeds within the dance environment which has been in practice from time immemorial.

Since most of the dance is between a man and a woman, biological friction is bound to take place. There is a chance that an active interaction between male and female might occur and this natural process can lead to either love or resentment. No one is here to tell you how to handle biological businesses. This game between a man and a woman has been on for thousands of years. It can be a beautiful thing if both parties handle it maturely. However, it can be very ugly if you don't play it right. Learn the art of love, yes it is an art. NO simply means NO! You don't force your way through the person, male or female.

When you learn the art of love, you will know how to love, how to be kind, and how to be gentle even in the middle of rejections.

Guys, we are naturally the leaders. That doesn't mean that we are above the followers. This is a major role to play. Ladies need to feel safe when in a close embrace and feel safe that, we are all there to protect them in the settings.

Ladies and gentlemen, I am not saying that you shouldn't have an affair with someone, but if you have the chance to do so, make sure it's a mutual consent and handle it gracefully. This can be a beautiful thing if you handle it well.

Live your life just the way you want it and enjoy living it, as long as you are straight with yourself, most likely, you will not hurt anybody who is truthful to themselves.

Ladies if a guy didn't pay attention to you, it doesn't mean there's something wrong with you. He is probably being fed well at home or he has his attention on someone else. Try not to have false expectations of him, because he might not fulfill it for you. You don't have to resent him because of that.

Guys, there is an abundance of beautiful women all around, whether in the social setting or somewhere at the bar or on the streets. There's no need to rush/rattle anybody. You will always have your chances if you act right.

It is not my obligation to be a moral adviser on how to handle your business but this is a true living reality in the social and festivals and as a matter of fact, you are going to be dealing with similar situations in your lifetime. Its better you learn it soon if not already, maybe through dancing. There are a lot of lessons to learn when you start social dancing beside dance itself. It is worth giving it a try; you might learn about con- fidence, romance, rejection, love, forgiveness, hygiene, communication especially non-verbal, and most importantly how to have fun. You pick a few tips and work on it. You will be amazed by your result.

Keep your eye on the goal, which should be your dance skills, and have fun along on the journey.

Guys, we are not there to hunt like a tiger, running around just to find someone to catch. That being said, if a lady says no to your invitation, whether is asking for her number for a date or just trying to dance more intimately like Tarrachinha dance (a dance drive from kizomba), Sensual Bachata respect her conclusion, you should never make any lady uncomfortable on the dance floor. They are there to have fun, and ladies trust you guys to lead them. That simply means responsibilities on your hands.

You can do all your fancy styles, turn, dips flip what have you and most of them won't complain. If she said no to some of your gesture, you need to respect it. Learn to take rejection gracefully. Don't be a creep by trying to follow her through- out the night. Keep in mind that, there are a lot of ladies on the social dance floor if she says no, the other lady might say differently. You shouldn't be trying to chase many ladies on the dance floor that will really be creepy. With enough patients, the right flower would lay on your arms in time.

You should just come with no high expectation on the social dance floor. You should come to just have fun and things will happen naturally with the right manners. Realize that if you just come to dance floor just to dance, you will actually enjoy this hobby. You can build great relationships with people and maintain good ones.

Do's And Don'ts

Fighting,

The social dancing event is one of the most peaceful and joyful places to be. Most of the dancers are classy and drama free. You will rarely see a drunken head on the dance floor. A lot of fight sparks in the local bars are due to people drinking above their alcoholic limits.

Unlike local bars, partner dance focuses on sharing the joy of dance with everyone in the building. Most social dancers are at least twenty -one year old and up to sixty-plus years old and this provides an atmosphere of mature people. The graceful atmosphere is maintained at all times.

In an effort to maintain this peaceful environment, fighting has no exception. This is something you should never attempt to spark. Even if someone steps on your foot, be the wise one and walk away.

In North America and Europe, if you spark a physical fight with someone, law enforcement will be involved. This process can cost you a lot of time and money. Moreover, you might ruin your reputation in the dance communities. Keep in mind that the internet has made it easier to keep these communities together and they are quick to spread out the certain news. Your unwelcome behaviors should be left at your door- step before you head out to social dancing. Once you are at the dance floor, switch to a social mode, dance, and share, forgive and have fun. Dance your problems away.

Sticking To One Dance Partner Or Not Rotating

This can be a complete turn off and inconsiderate. Rotation (dance wheel) is there to try to balance out the dance experience with everyone on the dance floor. That's why we switch from one partner to the other after a certain amount of songs. Sticking with only one dance partner for many songs in a row is not helpful to the dance wheel. There is no general rule to how many songs in a row you should dance with one partner. It is mainly about you using your common senses to access the situation. However, you may keep these general rules as a guideline. Ballroom dances have their own rotational rules but dances such as Bachata, Kizomba, Salsa, Zouk have a different expectations to how you should rotate.

In social setting for Bachata, Kizomba, Salsa, Zouk especially in local bars, pubs, studios, try to keep your dance in between one song to three songs the most for one partner. Three songs in a row are sufficient enough to build dance chemistry with a dancer. Dance chemistry occurs when you know how to adapt to your partner. You quickly learn what level the dancer is and finding a way to balance it. If you are a veteran dancer, within the first one minute of the songs you can build dance chemistry.

At festival settings, you may bump it up to four songs with one partner if you like. Since the Djs fade out some songs before it finishes. You should pace yourself, especially at the dance festivals, because most festivals have three to four night of social dancing, in addition to classes and mini parties. You will have enough time to dance with a lot of dancers.

Ladies if you are dancing with a guy and he passes six songs in a row, you might need to tell him thank you for the dance and move on with someone else. Some guys don't know how it works. So your help is highly needed. Since ladies usually outnumber the guys, it can help the guys to keep up with the dance wheel. Ladies don't like waiting for so long without a dance, especially if they wear that lovely shoe. Common sense rotation will help to solve that problem.

Stealing Purses and People's Belongings

Whenever you have too many people on one floor, definitely you can find certain people who are not straight with themselves. Some may definitely take advantage of situations and trespass on people's belongings. This rarely happens on a mini socialist in the communities, because most people know each other and they respect their friends' belongings.

That being said, festival settings, keep your eye on your belongings. Not all the people there are genuine dancers, who respect the rules of social dancing and the environment. It's very important as a dancer to take precautions and also never participate in such actions. Try to bring items to the socials that can easily be replaced when lost. Avoid bringing personal belongings to the festival socials such as wallet, I.D or passports. If you are traveling overseas for a festival, definitely keep your passport in the right place. Losing that can be challenging, on a side note, take a picture of your passport, email yourself with the passport picture. This will save it in your email history. And make a colored copy of it. Keep the copy in a separate bag. In case you lose your passport, you can take the copy to the nearest embassy to get a temporary solution. You can also keep those items at your hotel room. Or guide it to hotel receptionist. Most hotels have free storage services available to the guests.

The belongings you may bring to the festival social room can be your phone, dance shoe in a small dance shoe bags. The bag with your normal shoe can be kept on the side or corner of the dance floor, that way you can keep your eye on it now and then. You can keep your phone in the back pocket of your pant if you have one. If that is not a safe option, add your phone with your other shoe in the shoe bag and guard it by the Dj booth. Let the Dj know to keep a glance on it for you. If you don't have anything too valuable on the shoe bag, you can get away by placing it on the side or corner on the dance floor.

I have never been a victim of lost or stolen item in any social or festival, and most of my friend have the same experience since I started social dancing in 2011. The chances of someone purposely stealing your belonging are slim. As I am writing this book, just recently in 2017 one of the prominent social dancer in the community once posted a Facebook post, " that someone has stolen her purse, including her credit card, money and all the stuff that come with the purse' As you can see she wasn't pleased with that at all. And no one should. And no one likes to feel violated. It is a disempowering feeling when an unknown person invades your privacy. It can change your whole mood in the social or festival. Social dancing is known to be a safe place for everyone, and help us keep it that way. People will take advantage of an open situation. Don't give them a chance.

Too Much Teaching on the Dance Floor

The way you approach classes and workshops should be completely different from the way you approach social settings. This is a big factor to always consider; you can completely change your dance partner's mood from pleasant to unpleasant when you decide to teach them in the middle of the social, even though you may be trying to help the dancer. He or she might interpret your suggestion differently. Try to enjoy the dance whether he or she is a great dancer or not.

Learn to switch mode base on the setting. Practice-mode is for practice, and the social-mode is for fun.

Social-Mode

Avoid teaching in social settings, unless if your partner is completely new and you just want to show him or her quick simple basic to follow. And that can be done effortlessly. The social settings are just for having fun. When someone really wants to learn to dance, direct them to the local instructor in the community. It is very important to know what mode you switch on and off when dancing, and which settings to use. It can be a big turn-off if you're dancing in a social setting and someone is trying to teach you how to do a particular move, and you are not up for it. It can be conflicting because you are not on the same page, one of you is in social mode and the other in the practice mode.

Dance life has a chain of a cycle. That's: you go to class to learn a particular dance. Next, you go out in the social setting to apply your knowledge in a more fun way. Then you go and take more classes and workshops to get better, and you go to social settings again and festivals to share dance skills with many people while having fun.

As you can see, there is a place for social and classes. Know when to practice and when to have fun.

Practice-Mode

In practice mode, this can either be in a class, workshop, or even a private session with a known instructor. When you are in this mode, your main goal is to learn something new in other to be better at particular movement or style of dancing. Your mind is fully engaged to get better, learn and grow. This is where you don't worry too much about having fun but just learning about getting better. You allow constructive criticism.

This is where you challenge yourself; you use a lot of memory tricks and counting to understand the movement. In his mode, it only becomes fun when you learn something new because once you master a particular dance and movement the Joy flows naturally. It is in our nature to get excited when we learn a new thing. That is one of the great things about dancing, there is always something to learn, and it is endlessly expanding like our cosmos. You will never get bored if you are willing to learn. To be a great dancer you must spend a lot of time in practice mode.

Avoid Being Too Loud

When on a dance floor, it is ok to chat with a friend for about five minutes or so, and then try to find your way to the dance floor. Just chatting and watching is not the essence of social dancing. You will find some folks on the dance floor talking out loud endlessly; try not to imbibe that habit. Once you paid your money to dance, get your pennyworth by engaging on the dance floor with dancers. Dance and rotate with a different partner as possible as you can. If someone is trying to talk you off, tell them to let continue this later and go do your dancing.

Talking out loud on the social dance floor can be seen as rude, disrespectful to the music and the floor, with no regards to others dancers. Respect the dance, respect the music, respect the floor and finally respect your dance partner.

Do Not Try To Force Her to Dance With You

Persuade a person instead of using intense pressure. Sometimes people will tell you no to a dance invitation. This doesn't mean he or she dislikes you. Unless if the dancer blatantly snubs your invitation and go on dancing with someone else right away. That should be prevented and reported to the event organizer. Know that it has nothing to do with you but a lot do with the invitee.

Besides prejudice rejection, there could be a lot of different valid reason for the person not willing to dance with you. It may not be about you. Don't get salty about it. When you have been social dancing for a while, you will figure out ways around certain rejection.

If someone says no to your invitation, you can follow these steps to figure out or persuade him or her especially if they are new dancers.

One of the most common reasons a person might say no to your dance request is that they are a new dancer and they don't want to look bad.

With this kind of challenge, it is easier to win over depending on how you handle it. For example guys, you have extended your hand to a lady, and said: "shall we dance"? And she responded "no" and said to you "I don't know how to dance this... Or I am a new dancer" You shouldn't give up. If you do, the new dancer might not have enough dances for the night to encourage her to come to the next social. Instead, smile and say something cool like this, "I am new too... let's figure it out together"... and lead her gently into basic moves. After the dance, tell her "we did it, and you did great! Keep it up". This approach will have great success with a newbie. But if she clearly rejects your persuasiveness, don't take it personally, it could be she was taking a rest, or she is not feeling good at that moment or something came up. There may be many reasons for rejections just try to avoid judging right away and Keep on moving to next available partner.

Part 11

Other Dance Events To Attend

Social Dance Congress

ADance Congress can be likened to a dance buffet where hundreds to thousands of dance lovers come to learn and share their love for dance. Dance congresses consist of performances, workshops, social dancing, and competitions. The competitions are based on a particular dance that the Congress is focused on.

A congress can be identified by its full name which is evident in names such as NYC Salsa Congress, Atlanta Kizomba Congress etc. and at times, the center focus of the Congress can be found by the name of the Congress. For example, in the Atlanta Kizomba congress the main focus is simply Kizomba, same also applies to the NYC salsa Congress where the main focus is Salsa dance. Sometimes the name of the congress has nothing to do with the dances, but the fine prints will indicate the dances involved. However, many of these congresses incorporate several sub dances such as Bachata, in fact, most of the salsa congresses have a lot of Bachata dance as part of the Congress.

Sometimes, it might be more than one sub dance included such as Zouk, Kizomba, and Tango. These sub dances also comes with instructors teaching workshops and their dedicated social dancing rooms. These congresses have many different workshops to learn from a multitude of instructors with many of them being world class dancers. It brings a surreal feeling to the dancing enthusiasts to learn from the masters of these Sub dances. The duration of a Dance Congress usually takes Multiples days to a week and a dance congress does not only provide a platform to learn from masters, but also watch live performances. Live Performances such as choreograph dance pattern by groups and even known musical Artists are common.

Social Dance Festivals

There is a great similarity between dance congress and festivals; which includes a gathering where a lot of workshops, social dancing, and performances are held. The main difference between a festival and a Congress is the size and the option of competition for dancers; dance festivals are often smaller in size and focuses more on workshops and social dancing. This is like your "one stop shop" for all your dancing needs and is a great way to experience different dances in a fun friendly environment. In a dance festival, you will find instructors of different backgrounds teaching, Bachata, Kizomba, Salsa, Zouk, Afrobeats and more. These events are usually the whole weekend, from Friday to Sunday. Almost every major city in the USA has at least a social dance festival or Congress in a year. You can identify a dance festival by its names, examples are the Orlando Salsa, Bachata Festival and Miami Beach Kizomba festival etc. it is important to note that some festivals are solely focused on one major dance. A research should be carried out before the festival from the festival's website where you can find full details about the festival; Information such as the date, time artist or instructor's lineup and festival timetable or day to day schedules.

Festivals are a great way of meeting international instructors and making new friends from different places. Preparation is important if you plan to attend a festival or congress in order to get the most out of it. Since there are a lot of professionals instructors available to you, you have great opportunities to take their classes and even schedule a private class with them. This can enhance your dance skills tremendously. One weekend at a festival is a super boost to your dance skills.

However, there are certain things to note, without proper planning a festival can be costly and exhausting, some of the expenditures to consider are:

- Tickets

- Lodging

- Transportation (air or land, if out of state)

- Food

- Private class (If you plan to take one, which is highly recommended)

- Your valuable time (if you work, you may need a time off)

This expenditure goes up and down depending on which festival it is. You need to plan properly, if not, at the end of the weekend, you may find yourself going through your savings. Consider what you need by asking similar questions.

1. What technique and skill you want to improve on?

2. Which instructors are teaching these techniques?

3. Do you like the instructor's styles and level of competency in other to take a private class with them?

4. Do you need to buy dance wears, such as leggings and shoe, if so how much are you willing to spend? How many dance festivals do you want to attend this year?

5. Which festivals and why?

These questions and other related ones are very important to ask before you purchase your ticket to a festival. If you don't have targeted goals toward a festival, you might end up feeling empty due to the time and money invested.

After the festival or congress, ask these questions.

Did you feel like you got your money's worth? If no, ask why? Is it you or the festival that failed to deliver as promised?

A lot of festivals will deliver the instructors and DJ lineups. At the end of the day, it is up to you the dancer to have a clear goal/target to achieve at the festival and try to reach it. Hopping from one festival to another without a clear goal can be unfulfilling, exhausting, costly. In the time it might get old on you quickly. If social dancing is a lifetime journey for you, milk it! Pace yourself. Enjoy a couple of festival in a year and plan for the next year.

What to expect in a festival and Congress

Most festivals start from Thursday through Sunday, 10 a.m. - 6 p.m. for the workshops. After 6 pm, the social dancing continues during the night. Sometimes day parties (Matinee) are held as well.

Workshops are organized in a group format.

You will be learning with different students, dancers, instructors. The workshops should be categorized into Basic, Intermediate, and Advance classes. You have the option which level to choose. The classes are not restricted to a particular level of dancers. Instructors are trained not to stop anybody from attending their class. They are nice enough to let all the students enjoy the class. However, make sure you choose the right class. If you know you are a beginner, take the beginners or the basic class. You will get more out of that than taking an advanced class. When you take the wrong class, you might find yourself struggling hard, with no sense of progress. Take the right class base on your level. You will learn better and feel progressive. This, in turn, will boost your confidence.

While taking workshops, take mental notes of valuable information. Memos after the class, write it down in your notepad or on your phone. Many instructors usually do a demonstration, recap at the end of the class. At this moment you may get your phone and capture the demonstration for later use.

Later in the evening throughout the night, the party and social dancing begin. In such capacity of dancing, it is vital to learn to dance efficiently. One of the ways to be an efficient dancer is to consider taking small steps while dancing, this helps to pace yourself and the less dramatic your steps are the more the energy conserved.

Since you're going to be taking workshops during the morning, note that you do not have to take all the workshops, pick and choose what Workshop you are really interested in and take those classes. You can find schedules list or timetable within the festival that would help you plan better. You can even find this timetable on the website before you arrive.

When you take a lot of classes than necessary, you may end up burning yourself out for the night event. Choose your favorite classes and take those ones. A proper planning and time management is the key to enjoying an extended weekend festival.

Since you might be in a different city, you might like to explore the city as well during your stay. If so, go through the timetable of the festival, and plan perfectly what you want to do there. Base on the breaks you have on your timetable, you may explore the restaurant life or other interest in that city. This is best done with a friend.

Get Energy By Taking Naps

Take naps, a nap is a source of energy. Naps are your best friends to rejuvenate your body. Don't worry about sleeping the whole seven to eight hours, which will not work here. Plan to take a couple of hours nap. Two to four hours naps can take you a long way.

For example, during the three days festival and your first class starts at 10 a.m. with your last class stopping at 2 p.m., it is advised to take a nap after the last class. What to eat must also be considered, and I suggest eating healthy foods due to Junks taking a longer time to digest because eating Junks will get you tired very easily and sleepy. Take naps before you eat, it has been proven to help you sleep better with less digestion in your system.

Next, if there is no an evening pool party at the festival. You can use that time to explore the city or take private classes.

The night dance parties usually start at ten p.m. all the way to four a.m. and usually don't get jamming until midnight. This gives you the opportunity to take a nap if you need to.

After the pool party or matinee, if there is one, in between nine p.m. to 11 p.m. This is a free time for naps or dinner. Take advantage of it before the night social.

Sometime congresses will have performances between eight pm to ten pm. Most festivals don't have large performances, if they do, it will be on during the social. Around eleven pm to one am.

What to wear & bring to a festival or congress

Let's divide it into workshops, pool party, and night party.

Workshops do not require any fancy outfits, ladies you can usually get away with leggings and any shirt t-shirts that you prefer. Since in the workshops you might get too involved and sweaty, it advisable to bring a small handkerchief to dry off the sweat.

Ladies have proper dance shoe for the particular dance. If it is a Bachata, Kizomba, Salsa,

Zouk workshop, get a Latin dance shoe. However, not all workshops require Latin dance shoe. Sometimes intensive class such as Afro-beat will require sneakers. Have the right shoe base on the class.

After the workshops, if there is a pool party in the evenings. It usually begins at six p.m. It may continue till 8 pm. The pool parties are similar to the spring break but with a lot of matured people, less drama, and just mad fun times. During the pool party, there will be a live DJ entertaining the crowd with people are jumping in and out of the pool. The whole vibe is just all about a good time which will suit water lovers and make sure you are prepared for it i.e. get all your proper gears as needed. Gears such as bathing suit, sandals, shorts, sunglass, sunscreen, towels (hotels do provide a bunch of clean towels too). The pool party can really be fun and wild. Don't be afraid of being truly you. Take the mask off and go wild. Trust me it can be an eye-opening experience. Just get out there, have fun, dance with many dancers.

It's a common practice to have line dance at pool parties. This gives you a moment to get your groove on with Merengue, Reggaeton, and afro- house music house music. Don't hesitate to challenge your feet with a bunch of dance fanatics.

Night social party, this is where you freshen up for your favorite outfit. Get you nice dance shoe and get ready to dance for many hours. The social night is the one you try to present yourself well. It contains the maximum number of attendees. Dress to impress if you want and don't forget to smell pleasant.

Tips For Saving Money

Room Sharing

Most of the festivals are hosted in the hotel. There are some that are cruise based. Wherever it may be, if you want to save money and still have fun, consider sharing the experience with somebody as a roommate. You can rent a hotel where the festival is hosted. Or you can even rent a house close to the festival through Airbnb or other sources. Some hotels allow up to four people in two double beds, and some have their own rules. Check with the hotel regulation and see how many people are allowed in one room. By sharing your room, there is less privacy kindly consider what works for you.

Choosing between renting in the hotel where the festival is hosted and renting a place through an Airbnb.

Based on my personal experience, it can be more convenient to rent a room at the hotel where the festival is located, especially if you are traveling out of town. You don't have to worry about commute back and forth to the hotel for the event. Once you in the hotel everything is there unless you want to step out for some personal reasons. Just commuting back and forth to the hotel and can be costly. The room services at the hotel are ideal. You are a phone call away from full services.

Furthermore, if you find a very great deal on Airbnb close to the venue, it might be an option to consider. Sometimes you get a very good deal on Airbnb, 1, 2, 3 bedrooms with kitchen and a nice comfortable house. When you are traveling with friends, you can split the expenses. This can be a good option base on your preference. Always make sure that the location is close to the venue so that you don't have to spend a lot of time and money going back and forth between the two locations.

Carpool With Friends

Another way of saving money is to carpool. If the festival is not too far from your city, let's say is probably less than 300 miles away. You may hit the road with a bunch of your friends. Simply get an affordable rental car and get a couple of friends that are willing to drive with you and split the cost evenly. This might be cheaper than a flight and you may have a quality time along the road with your friends. Just make sure they are the people that you prefer around you, it's a lot more fun that way.

Buy Ticket In Advance Or On Sales

You can also save a lot of money by buying your tickets in advance. Many festivals organizers have promotional sales at holidays such as Christmas, and Labor Days in advance. Buying on sale and early can save you some cash. Check the festival Facebook page to catch those promotional dates. Also, some festivals have affiliate marketing that sells the ticket at a discounted rate. You can check your local dance instructors or well-known dances for such deals.

Be A Promoter

Another way to save money on your ticket is to be a promoter for the festival, consult with the organizers of the festival, and they'll give you the requirements. Sometimes you have to sell up to five or more tickets in order to get a free pass. And after that amount, you actually get paid a certain percentage for selling those tickets. As a promoter, make sure you have a code that is traceable, and you really get paid for your effort. If your organizer is not straight with him, you might not get paid your effort. A good promoter can make some extra income, to pay for your ticket and your Hotel expenses while you are there.

Volunteer

Another great option is to volunteer for the festival. All festivals have their requirements.

Check with them before making a decision. Most volunteers are assigned to do a regular day-to- day operation of the festival. They do take turns, so you might not be in bondage; there is still little freedom to experience everything in the festival, as long as it is not your turn to volunteer.

Other Things to Consider

Food

For food instead of buying at the venue, it might be more affordable trying to local restaurants, especially mom-and-pop corner restaurants.

These restaurants can be very affordable and a nice way of trying the local authentic food. To find one, ask one of the hotel employees, they may have you a good recommendation. Eating at the hotel restaurant can be expensive and not quite authentic local type.

How to Schedule Privates With Professionals

Most of the instructors at the festivals are well known around the dance world. Some of them are international renounce instructors and dancers. It will be smart to schedule a private with them while they are there with you.

If you're interested in taking private with the instructor that you like, simply ask them right after the workshop. He or she will let you know their availability and price per hour. Common private price ranges $80-$150; it depends on the competency and popularity of the instructors. Don't be afraid to bargain if it seems too pricey for you. Knocking out to $10 to$15 of the quoted $120 or $150 can be used as lunch money. A private class is a great way to enhance your dance skills. The instructor can easily transfer his or her knowledge to you directly. The instructor can easily scan your dance skills and provide tips for improvement. Plan to set money aside for private if you want to take. Private also encourages and support the instructors to keep doing what they love to do. Be a Good Samaritan and support the Dance Movement. While gaining skills and enhancing your lifestyles.

Professionalism - Respect The Instructor

Every instruction has their own way of teaching, such as every person is unique and every dance has their own unique personality. Taking a class from an instructor, whether at a festival or just regular class, is respectful. During classes avoid being too loud while instructors are teaching. If you have any question or doubt just raise your hand and ask the question. If you don't like what the instructor teaches, just remember it's only hour class; you wouldn't be there for more than that anyway.

Vendors

Some festivals and Congress have vendors with tents to sell dance related items. Some of the vendors' sales, jewelry, artworks, shirts, and dance shoes, Festivals are a great place to buy your first pair of dance shoes. You can try them on. Test it out and see how it fits. Other common items that can be found at dance festival are jumpsuit for ladies. You may also found booth on other upcoming festivals this can be a great way to get a promotional price for your nest festival.

Thank you so much, I hope this book has been helpful to you, and keep on dancing joyfully!

37705631R00095

Printed in Great Britain
by Amazon